CHILDCRAFT
THE HOW AND WHY LIBRARY

CELEBRATE!

World Book, Inc.
a Scott Fetzer company
Chicago

Childcraft—The How and Why Library

© 2007 World Book, Inc. All rights reserved. This volume may not be reproduced in whole or in part in any form without prior written permission from the publisher.

CHILDCRAFT, CHILDCRAFT—THE HOW AND WHY LIBRARY, HOW AND WHY, WORLD BOOK and the GLOBE DEVICE are registered trademarks or trademarks of World Book, Inc.

World Book, Inc.
233 N. Michigan Avenue
Chicago, IL 60601

Previous editions © 2004, 2000, 1996-1993, 1991-1989, 1987-1985 World Book, Inc.; © 1982-1979 World Book-Childcraft International, Inc.; © 1976, 1974-1973, 1971-1968, 1965-1964 Field Enterprises Educational Corporation; International Copyright © 2000, 1996-1993, 1991-1989, 1987-1985, World Book, Inc.; © 1982-1979 World Book-Childcraft International, Inc.; © 1976, 1974-1973, 1971-1968, 1965-1964 Field Enterprises Educational Corporation. All rights reserved.

The Library of Congress has cataloged a previous edition of this title as follows.

Childcraft: the how and why library.
    v. cm.
   Summary: Presents illustrated articles, stories, and poems, grouped thematically in fifteen volumes.
    Includes bibliographical references and indexes.
    Contents: v. 1. Poems and rhymes -- v. 2. Once upon a time -- v. 3. Art around us -- v. 4. The world of animals -- v. 5 The world of plants -- v. 6. Our earth -- v. 7. The universe -- v. 8. How does it happen? -- v. 9. How things work -- v. 10. Shapes and numbers -- v. 11. About you -- v. 12. Who we are -- v. 13. See the world -- v. 14. Celebrate! -- v. 15. Guide and index.
    ISBN 0-7166-2203-3 (set)
    1. Children's encyclopedias and dictionaries.
[1. Encyclopedias and dictionaries.] 1. Title: Childcraft.
II. World Book, Inc.
AG6 .C48 2004
031--dc21   2003008722

This edition:

ISBN-13: 978-0-7166-2219-2 (set)
ISBN-10: 0-7166-2219-X (set)
ISBN-13: 978-0-7166-2233-8 (Volume 14, Celebrate!)
ISBN-10: 0-7166-2233-5 (Volume 14, Celebrate!)

Printed in China
4 5 6 7 8 9 09 08 07 06

For information on other World Book publications, visit our Web site at **http://www.worldbook.com** or call **1-800 WORLDBK (967-5325)**. For information on sales to schools and libraries, call **1-800-975-3250 (United States)**, or **1-800-837-5365 (Canada)**.

Contents

People celebrate for many reasons. We mark our special days on a calendar. But did you know that not everybody has the same calendar?

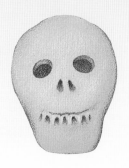

Introduction

This book is all about the many kinds of holidays and events that people celebrate around the world. Some celebrations mark the passing of the year and the changing of the seasons. Some are national holidays, and others are religious holidays. Still other celebrations honor people, such as kings and queens, national heroes, religious leaders, soldiers, parents, and working people. Your own birthday is also a reason for celebration!

Starting with January and ending with December, each chapter begins with a calendar filled with names and descriptions of famous people who have birthdays that month. Be sure to look up your own birthday and see who shares that date with you! You will also find out what sorts of celebrations take place in various parts of the world during each month. Some holidays are celebrated with quiet prayer, while many others are celebrated with lively parties and colorful parades or fireworks.

There are many features in this book to help you find your way through it. The boxes marked **Know It All!** have fun-filled facts. You can amaze your friends with what you learn!

This book also has many activities that you can do at home. Look for the words **Try This!** over a colored ball. The activity that follows offers a way to learn more about a celebration. For example, you can make sweet rice cakes, a snow leopard mask, a carp kite, or a paper cat.

Each activity has a number in its colored ball. Activities with a 1 in a green

Know It All! boxes have fun-filled facts.

Each activity has a number. The higher the number, the more adult help you may need.

An activity that has this colorful border is a little more complex than one without the border.

ball are simplest to do. Those with a 2 inside a yellow ball may require a little adult help with tasks such as cutting or measuring. Activities with a 3 inside a red ball may need more adult help.

A Try This! activity that has a colorful border around its entire page is a little more complex or requires a few more materials. Take a moment to review the list of materials and to read through the instructions before you begin.

As you read this book, you will see that some words are printed in bold type, **like this.** These are words that might be new to you. You can find the meanings and pronunciations of these words in the **Glossary.** Turn to the **Index** to look up page numbers of subjects that interest you the most.

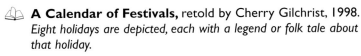

If you enjoy learning about celebrations, find out more about them in other resources, such as those listed below. Check them out at a bookstore or at the library in your school or town.

📖 **A Calendar of Festivals,** retold by Cherry Gilchrist, 1998. *Eight holidays are depicted, each with a legend or folk tale about that holiday.*

📖 **Celebrating Chinese New Year,** by Diane Hoyt-Goldsmith, 1999. *A young boy and his family prepare for and celebrate the most important holiday of their year.*

📖 **Children Just Like Me: Celebrations,** by Anabel and Barnabas Kindersley, 1997. *Meet children from around the world and learn how they celebrate 25 of their favorite holidays and traditions.*

📖 **Festivals of the World: Netherlands,** by Joyce van Fenema, 1998. *Explore the festivals and culture of this area. Check out other books in the "Festivals of the World" series.*

📖 **The First Thanksgiving,** by Jean Craighead George, 1996. *This award-winning author tells the story of the Green Corn Dance, the Harvest Feast, and the First Thanksgiving.*

📖 **Harvest Celebrations,** by Clare Chandler, 1998. *Harvest festivals occur around the world to celebrate a successful crop, and you can read about those festivals in this book.*

🌐 **Holidays Around the World,** http://www.yahooligans.com/Around_the_World/Holidays/ *This is a starting place to get more information on holidays.*

📖 **Let's Celebrate Valentine's Day,** by Peter and Connie Roop, 1999. *Make a valentine pop-up card and sugar cookies, and learn about the history and customs of this holiday.*

📖 **Mardi Gras,** by Dianne M. MacMillan, 1997. *Learn the history and customs of Mardi Gras.*

📖 **Memorial Day,** by Mir Tamim Ansary, 2002. *This beautifully illustrated book is just one in the "Holiday Histories" series.*

📖 **The Menorah Story,** by Mark Podwal, 1998. *This story of Hanukkah and the menorah is told in a simple style.*

📖 **St. Patrick's Day,** by Gail Gibbons, 1995. *Simple text and brightly colored illustrations give the background of this holiday.*

📖 **World Book's Christmas Around the World series.** *Each volume in this series describes Christmas customs, crafts, and recipes in a different country or region.*

What's a Celebration?

People celebrate for many reasons. Some people celebrate special family days. Other people get together as a group, a community, or even as a whole nation to celebrate a special event. Many celebrations are religious. People also celebrate certain times of the year.

Some celebrations take place on days when you don't have to go to school and adults don't have to go to work. These days are often marked with visits from friends and relatives and with special treats. Sometimes, people have picnics. And sometimes, people go to a church, a temple, or another house of worship.

What Do People Celebrate?

Some of our festivals and celebrations mark the passing of the year and its changing seasons. These are usually very old customs. Long, long ago, before people had heating and electric lights, winter in many places was a hard time of dark days and bad weather. No wonder people celebrated the coming of summer with feasting and dancing! A good harvest at the end of the summer meant that there would be plenty to eat all winter. Everyone gave thanks for good crops.

Birthdays are favorite celebrations for many people. It's fun to have a birthday cake with candles on it—one candle for every year of your life. Some people get birthday presents. Some people have a birthday party and invite all their friends.

Many people celebrate the birthday of their country. People also often celebrate the birthdays of religious leaders, presidents, kings and queens, national heroes, or other people they want to remember and honor.

Some holidays honor special groups of people. For example, certain days remind us of those who died fighting for their country. On other days, we honor people we love and respect, such as our parents and our teachers. A few holidays honor working people.

Some **Christians** celebrate "name days." In some countries, children are named after Christian **saints**. Each saint has a special day, and children named after a saint celebrate on that saint's day.

The word *holiday* comes from the words *holy day*—a day on which people pray or give thanks. Some holy days are celebrated by people all around the world. These important days may be remembered by going to a place of worship, by gathering together to pray, or by dressing up and having a good time. Some of the celebrations include feasting or a time of **fasting**. Fasting means that people stop eating, eat less than usual, or stop eating certain things.

Some celebrations are holidays, but not all of them. Today, we use the word *holiday* for any day of celebration, relaxation, or other change from an ordinary day.

On holidays, you may see parades with marching bands. At night, there may be dazzling fireworks.

Holidays are filled with traditions. People often prepare wonderful foods especially for holidays. People sometimes wear traditional clothing or brighten their homes and neighborhoods with holiday lights and decorations. People also sing traditional songs and play holiday games. What are some of your favorite traditions?

We sometimes celebrate days that seem to be just for fun. On some of these days, we play jokes on people. On others, we get together with friends and neighbors to enjoy music, dancing, and singing.

When People Celebrate?

How do you know what day a holiday falls on? You look at a calendar, of course! But long ago, the only "calendars" people had were the moon, the sun, the stars, and the changing seasons. Even today we still use calendars that follow the changes of the moon and the seasons.

People made the first calendars by dividing a year into 12 "moons," or months. But they had a problem. A year is the time it takes the earth to travel once around the sun. This comes to about 365 days. A

moon-month is the time from one new moon to the next—about 29 1/2 days. There are 12 months in a year. So 12 moon-months come to about 354 days. And this is 11 days less than a year!

Sometimes people added days or months to keep the calendar in step with the seasons. Over the years, some people developed a calendar that matched the seasons. They based this calendar on the solar year, or the time it takes for the earth to circle the sun. It has 365 days.

How many days are in each month? Here's a quick way to remember. Hold up the fingers of one hand, except for your thumb. Call your index finger January. Then slide down to the space between your fingers. That's February. Go to the next fingers and spaces for March, April, May, June, and July. Start over again for August. All the months that landed on fingertips have 31 days. The rest have 30, except February which has even fewer.

KNOW It All!

These children in Greece are dressed in traditional clothes for an Easter celebration. Easter is a religious holiday. It is also a "floating holiday" that is always on a Sunday.

Holidays and Calendars

Some holidays follow calendars based on the moon. These days are called "floating holidays" because they float around on our standard calendar. They are not celebrated on the same day each year. Many of these floating holidays are religious. They follow a religious calendar.

The Chinese calendar

The Chinese calendar follows the moon. But it also groups years into sets of 12. Each year is named for an animal. The first of the twelve years is the Year of the Rat. This is followed by the years of the ox, tiger, hare, dragon, snake, horse, sheep, monkey, rooster, dog, and pig.

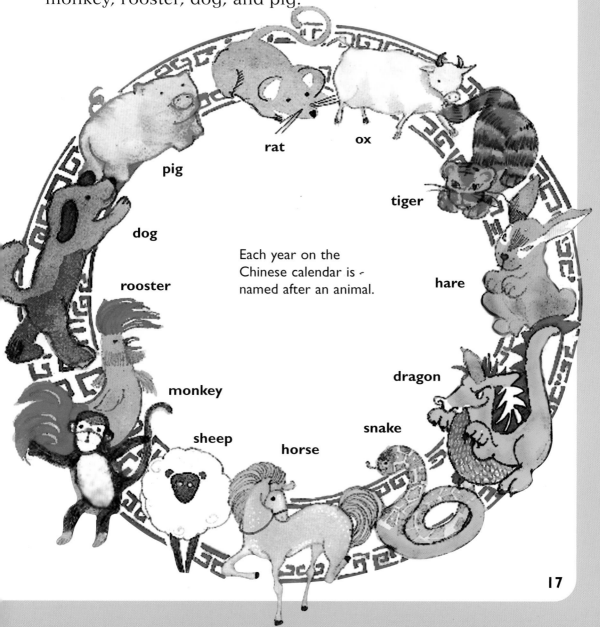

rat

ox

pig

tiger

dog

rooster

Each year on the Chinese calendar is named after an animal.

hare

dragon

monkey

snake

sheep

horse

The Hebrew Calendar

The Hebrew, or Jewish, calendar is also based on the moon. The **Jews** use it to fix the dates of their religious years. There are 12 months in the Hebrew calendar. An extra month, added seven times every 19 years, keeps the calendar more or less in time with the seasons. Also, days are added or taken away to make sure certain holy days fall on proper days of the week. As a result, a Jewish year can be as short as 353 days or as long as 385 days.

The Christian Calendar

Christian calendars use the moon to set some holy days, too. Easter, for example, can fall any time from March 22 through April 25. The exact date depends on the moon.

The Muslim Calendar

Muslims (MUHZ luhmz) follow the religion of Islam. They also use a calendar based on the moon. It has 12 months of 30 or 29 days. Eleven times in every 30 years, an extra day is added. This keeps the calendar in time with the moon, but not with the seasons.

The Islamic year is only 354 or 355 days long. It does not follow the calendar year that includes the months of January through December. That calendar year has 365 days. The Islamic year is about 11 days shorter than that. So each year, an Islamic holiday is about 11 days earlier than the year before. But in 32 1/2 years, it's back to where it started.

These pictures represent some of the famous people born in January. The numbers tell you the days on which they were born. Look at the calendar on the following pages to find out more.

The Month of January

In most of the world, January is the first month of the year. It is named after the ancient Roman god Janus (JAY nuhs).

Janus was the god of beginnings and the god of gates and doorways. He is shown with two faces. One face looks to the future. The other face looks back at the past.

In the northern part of the world, January is cold and snowy. It is near the beginning of winter. People go skating and sledding. But in the southern part of the world, January is warm. It is near the beginning of summer— a time for swimming and picnics.

22

25

January

Who Shares My Birthday?

Is your birthday in January? This calendar shows the names of some famous people born in January. What do you know about the people who share your birthday?

1
Paul Revere (1735) hero of the American Revolution

Betsy Ross (1752) American flagmaker

Manuel Roxas y Acuña (1892) first president of Philippines

2
James Wolfe (1727) British general who won Canada for the British Empire

Isaac Asimov (1920) American biochemist and author

7
Millard Fillmore (1800) 13th President of the United States

Valery N. Kubasov (1935) Soviet cosmonaut who participated in first U.S.-Soviet joint space mission

8
Elvis Presley (1935) American rock music star

Stephen Hawking (1942) British scientist and author of *A Brief History of Time*

David Bowie (1947) British rock singer and actor

13
Salmon P. Chase (1808) antislavery leader

Horatio Alger (1832) American author of boys' books

Francis Everett Townsend (1867) American physician and social reformer

14
Albert Schweitzer (1875) German doctor and missionary

Hugh Lofting (1886) English author who wrote the "Doctor Dolittle" series

15
Molière (1622) French writer of plays who became known as the greatest French writer of comedies

Martin Luther King, Jr. (1929) American minister and civil rights leader

16
Robert W. Service (1874) Canadian "Poet of the Yukon"

Dian Fossey (1932) American scientist known for her studies of gorillas

18
Edmund Barton (1849) 1st prime minister of Australia

Rubén Darío (1867) Nicaraguan poet and political leader

A. A. Milne (1882) English author who wrote *Winnie-the-Pooh*

19
Edgar Allan Poe (1809) American short-story writer and poet who wrote "The Raven"

Javier Perez de Cuellar (1920) Peruvian secretary-general of the United Nations (UN) from 1982 to 1991

20
Joy Adamson (1910) Czech-born author of *Born Free*

Edwin Eugene "Buzz" Aldrin, Jr. (1930) American astronaut

21
Ethan Allen (1738) hero of the American Revolution who captured Fort Ticonderoga

Thomas "Stonewall" Jackson (1824) Confederate Army general during the Civil War

26
Mary Mapes Dodge (1831) American author who wrote *Hans Brinker*

Maria von Trapp (1905) Austrian leader of the Trapp Family Singers

27
Wolfgang Amadeus Mozart (1756) Austrian composer, one of the greats

Lewis Carroll (1832) English author of *Alice's Adventures in Wonderland*

3

Cicero (106 B.C.) Roman statesman and author

Lucretia Mott (1793) American Quaker and women's rights leader

J. R. R. Tolkien (1892) British author of *The Hobbit* and *The Lord of the Rings*

4

Jakob Grimm (1785) German collector of fairy tales

Louis Braille (1809) French inventor of a system of writing for the blind

5

Shah Jahan (1592) Indian ruler who built the Taj Mahal

Stephen Decatur (1779) American naval hero in the War of 1812

Alvin Ailey (1931) American choreographer

6

Joan of Arc (1412?) French heroine who led the French to victory

Jacques Étienne Montgolfier (1745) French inventor of hot-air balloon

Kim Dae Jung (1924) Korean politician who worked for human rights

9

Carrie Chapman Catt (1859) American leader in women's right-to-vote movement

George Balanchine (1904) Russian-born ballet choreographer

Richard M. Nixon (1913) 37th president of the United States

10

Ray Bolger (1904) American entertainer; played the scarecrow in *The Wizard of Oz*

11

Sir John A. MacDonald (1815) 1st prime minister of Canada

Jean Chrétien (1934) 26th prime minister of Canada

12

Charles Perrault (1628) French writer of fairy tales; known for *Tales of Mother Goose*

Pieter Willem Botha (1916) leader of South Africa's government from 1978 to 1989

16

17

17

17

Benjamin Franklin (1706) American statesman and inventor

Mack Sennett (1884) Canadian film director

Muhammad Ali (1942) American heavyweight boxing champion

22

Francis Bacon (1561) English philosopher, writer, and statesman

Lord Byron (1788) English poet

U Thant (1909) Burmese diplomat and secretary-general of the United Nations

23

John Hancock (1737) first signer of the U.S. Declaration of Independence

Edouard Manet (1832) French painter

Princess Caroline (1957) of Monaco, daughter of Grace Kelly and Prince Rainier

24

Edith Wharton (1862) American writer

Maria Tallchief (1925) American ballet star

Mary Lou Retton (1968) gymnast who became the most awarded U.S. athlete at the 1984 Olympics

25

Robert Burns (1759) Scottish poet

Antonio Carlos Jobim (1927) Brazilian composer of *bossa nova* dance music

Corazon Aquino (1933) first woman president of the Philippines

28

Alexander Mackenzie (1822) 2nd prime minister of Canada

Mikhail Baryshnikov (1948) Soviet-born ballet dancer and choreographer

29

William McKinley (1843) 25th President of the United States

Abdus Salam (1926) Pakistani scientist and 1979 Nobel Prize winner

30

George Bass (1771) British explorer of Australian coast

Franklin Roosevelt (1882) 32nd president of the United States

31

Anna Pavlova (1881) Russian ballet dancer

Jackie Robinson (1919) first African American player in major league baseball

New Year's Day

Shhhh! We're counting the seconds to midnight. The new year is almost here. As the clock begins to strike 12, noise fills the air in many parts of the world. Church bells ring out and people toot horns. Everyone shouts, "Happy New Year!"

Why is there so much noise? It's one way people show how happy they are. It's also an old custom. Long ago, people believed that loud noises scared away evil spirits.

Many people also celebrate New Year's Day with special customs. Some visit friends and relatives. Some make New Year's resolutions. They promise themselves to do better in the new year than they did in the old year.

Children in Belgium write their parents New Year's messages on decorated paper and read them on New Year's Day. In Russia, children may visit the Kremlin in the heart of Moscow. There, they see a huge fir tree called the New Year Tree. The tree is decorated with many colored lights.

In Scotland, the evening of December 31 is called Hogmanay (HAHG muh nay). People wait up on Hogmanay until

Grandfather Frost and his helper the Snow Maiden give New Year's gifts to children.

midnight for the "first footer" to arrive. The "first footer" is the first person to cross over the doorstep on the first day of the new year. According to Scottish **tradition,** the first footer carries a piece of coal to bring wealth, and a sprig of mistletoe to protect the family from the old year's spirits.

In Ecuador, people make a straw man dressed in their old clothes. They give the man a list of their family's faults, then burn him and the list at midnight to get rid of all their faults.

New Year's Day has been celebrated since ancient times. But it has not always been celebrated on January 1. Even today, people in many parts of the world begin their new year on other dates.

Jews celebrate their new year, Rosh Ha-Shanah, in September or October (see pages 140 and 141). The Chinese new year begins in January or February (see page 42).

In many parts of the world, people eat special foods to bring good luck in the coming year. In Japan, people eat a kind of pink fish called red snapper. Pink is a lucky color in Japan. In southern India, they boil new rice to bring good luck.

People in Tokyo, Japan, ring a giant bell at a temple to announce the new year. They ring the bell with a large log that they swing around by pulling on ropes.

In Portugal, people choose 12 grapes from a bunch. They eat them one by one as the clock strikes midnight.

In countries in Europe, roast pig is often served on New Year's Day. In Hungary, the pig has a four-leaf clover in its mouth for good luck.

In Romania, people stuff their pockets with corn. They walk from house to house "sowing" the corn by tossing it at friends to bring them good luck.

How do you welcome the new year? Try some of these ideas or make up some of your own!

Colorful parades are held each year on New Year's Day. This float shows aliens communicating with people on Earth.

Punch for the New Year

Ring in the new year with this tasty punch. The following directions make enough for about 15 cups.

What To Do:

1. Pour the ginger ale into the punch bowl.

2. Add the sherbet. Break up each scoop into smaller chunks.

3. Put in the ice cubes and stir. Add the orange slices for decoration.

4. Ladle the punch into cups and serve. Happy New Year!

You Will Need:

2 liters of ginger ale, chilled

6 scoops of raspberry or orange sherbet

1 unpeeled orange, cut in thin slices (ask an adult to help you)

10 ice cubes

a large punch bowl

paper cups

a ladle

Feast of Epiphany

In Italy, a kind old witch named Befana leaves children gifts on the Feast of Epiphany as she searches for the Christ child.

It is said that three wise men followed a guiding star to a stable in Bethlehem to see the baby Jesus. There, they gave the Christ child gifts of gold, **frankincense** (FRANG kihn sehns), and **myrrh** (mur).

With this story in mind, children in Puerto Rico fill their shoes with grass or straw just before bedtime on January 5. The grass or straw is for the animals ridden by the Three Wise Men, sometimes called the Three Kings. The next morning, known as the Feast of **Epiphany** (ih PIHF uh nee) or Three Kings' Day, the children find candy and toys in their shoes—gifts from the Three Kings.

KNOW It All!

The word *epiphany* means "appearance." Long ago, Christ's appearance on earth—his birth—was celebrated on the Feast of Epiphany. Today in Eastern churches, the Feast of Epiphany celebrates the baptism of Christ. In Western churches, it is a day to honor the visit of the Three Wise Men.

This Muslim family in the Middle East prepares special food for Ramadan.

Ramadan

Do people of your religion eat and drink less during certain times of the year? This is called **fasting. Muslims** (MUHZ luhmz), people who follow the Islamic religion, fast for a month every year.

Both the long fast and the month are called Ramadan (ram uh DAHN). This is the ninth month of the Islamic year. Because the Islamic calendar is based on the moon, the dates of Ramadan change. During the early 2000's, Ramadan occurs in autumn in the northern part of the world, but each year it moves a little earlier in the year.

During Ramadan, Muslims fast every day from dawn to sunset. They fast to have their sins forgiven. Those who cannot fast for some reason must either make up the days they miss or feed the hungry. Pregnant women, young children, the elderly, and people who are ill do not have to fast.

In the daytime, Muslims work less and spend more time praying and reading their holy book, called the **Quran** (ku RAHN).

Muslims celebrate the end of Ramadan with a great festival called the Festival of the Breaking of the Fast. It is one of the two great Muslim festivals. The other is the Festival of Sacrifice (see page 93).

These Muslims in Africa say special prayers for Ramadan.

Australia Day

January 26

32

Clink-clank-clink. Barefoot prisoners in chains trudge along the road. All around them are guards with guns.

These people aren't really prisoners and guards. They're part of a celebration that is held every year in Sydney, Australia's oldest and largest city. The marchers are showing people what life was like in Australia more than 200 years ago.

On January 26, 1788, a fleet of ships anchored in a harbor on the coast of Australia at what is now Sydney. These ships brought 730 prisoners from Britain. The prisoners, or convicts, were the first Europeans to settle in Australia. Since then, millions of Europeans have chosen Australia as their homeland. Wherever they're from, they all take part in celebrating Australia Day every year on the Monday closest to January 26.

On this national holiday, Australians enjoy folk dances and happy music from the many nations of people who now live in Australia. Dancers and musicians perform in the oldest part of Sydney, called the Rocks. This hilly area is near the harbor where the first Europeans landed.

On Australia Day, Australians act out the first landing at Sydney, the nation's oldest city. These actors are passing the Sydney Opera House.

Republic Day in India

Rose petals fall from the sky. Huge elephants wearing clanging bells and shining beads lumber down the street along with big, armored tanks. What a parade! It's Republic Day, a national holiday of India.

Republic Day, January 26, marks the date in 1950 when India had its own constitution, or set of basic laws. People in India celebrate this as a big step in their independence from Great Britain.

On Republic Day, celebrations occur all over India. The biggest celebration takes place in New Delhi, the capital city. There, a great parade travels down the Raj Path, or Government Road.

Many parades begin with rose petals being dropped from helicopters. Then bands begin to play and Indian soldiers called jawans (juh WAHNZ) march in perfect order. The parading elephants carry musicians wearing brightly colored turbans. As the parade ends, thousands of green, white, and orange-yellow balloons—the colors of India's flag—float into the air. For the next two days, folk dancers entertain crowds throughout New Delhi.

KNOW It All!

Another holiday that celebrates India's independence as a republic is Independence Day. It falls on August 15, the date India gained its independence from Great Britain in 1947.

> "I have a dream that my four little children will one day live in a nation where they will not be judged by the color of their skin but by the content of their character."

Martin Luther King, Jr., Day

Floating holiday

Martin Luther King, Jr., was a Baptist minister. He led people to work against the bad treatment that African Americans in the United States got in the mid-1900's. Until then, African Americans in many states were not allowed to go to the same schools as white people or buy houses in white neighborhoods. Blacks had to use different drinking fountains and sit in different areas of restaurants and movie theaters, too. Many were treated violently.

King wanted to change this unfair treatment. He preached that people must learn to live together and that people should not like or dislike others because of the color of their skin. He preached that violence is bad.

People threw stones at King and put him in jail for his words and actions. In 1968, a hidden rifleman shot and killed King.

Today, many people around the world have followed King's ideas. In the U.S., people honor King by celebrating Martin Luther King, Jr., Day on the third Monday in January.

TRY THIS!

1

Tell a friend or an adult why you think it is wrong to like people or not like people because of the color of their skin.

Martin Luther King, Jr., was one of the most famous civil rights leaders in history. In 1964, he received the Nobel Peace Prize for his nonviolent work.

These pictures represent some of the famous people born in February. The numbers tell you the days on which they were born. Look at the calendar on the following pages to find out more.

The Month of February

February is the second month of the year and the shortest. Usually, this month has only 28 days. But every fourth year—called leap year—an extra day is added. This keeps the calendar in time with the seasons. If you were born on February 29, you have a real birthday only once every four years.

The word *February* comes from the Latin word *februare,* which means "to purify" or "to make clean."

February is usually cold and stormy in the northern half of the world and warm and sunny in the south.

February

Who Shares My Birthday?

Is your birthday in February? This calendar shows the names of some of the famous people born in February. What do you know about the people who share your birthday?

1

Hattie Wyatt Caraway (1878) first woman elected to the U.S. Senate

Louis S. St. Laurent (1882) 17th prime minister of Canada

Langston Hughes (1902) American poet

2

Daniel Boone (1734) American pioneer and explorer

James Joyce (1882) Irish author who wrote *Ulysses*

Garth Brooks (1962) American country singer and superstar

4

7

Charles Dickens (1812) English author who wrote *A Christmas Carol*

Laura Ingalls Wilder (1867) American author best known for her "Little House" books

Russell Drysdale (1912) Australian artist known for his nature paintings

12

Charles Darwin (1809) British naturalist famous for theories on evolution

Abraham Lincoln (1809) 16th president of the United States

Judy Blume (1938) American author

13

Talleyrand (1754) French statesman under Napoleon I

Randolph Churchill (1849) British statesman and father of Winston Churchill

Grant Wood (1891) American painter

14

Jack Benny (1894) American entertainer

15

Galileo Galilei (1564) Italian astronomer

John Barrymore (1882) American movie actor

Norman Bridwell (1928) American author and illustrator of "Clifford" series

18

Mary I (1516) queen of England from 1553 to 1558

Toni Morrison (1931) American author and Nobel Prize winner who wrote *Beloved*

19

Nicolaus Copernicus (1473) Polish astronomer

Carson McCullers (1917) American author of *The Heart is a Lonely Hunter*

Prince Andrew (1960) second son of Queen Elizabeth

20

Angelina Grimke (1805) American who worked for women's rights and against slavery

Ansel Adams (1902) American landscape photographer

21

Alice Palmer (1855) American educator and college president

Barbara Jordan (1936) first African American woman member of U.S. Congress

Andres Segovia (1893) Spanish classical guitarist

26

Victor Hugo (1802) French author who wrote *The Hunchback of Notre Dame*

William Cody (1846) American frontiersman known as Buffalo Bill

27

22

29

3

Felix Mendelssohn (1809) German composer

Elizabeth Blackwell (1821) first woman doctor in the United States

Norman Rockwell (1894) American artist

4

Charles Lindbergh (1902) American aviator who was first to fly across the Atlantic alone

Rosa Lee Parks (1913) American civil rights leader known for her 1955 bus boycott

5

Sir Robert Peel (1788) British prime minister from 1834 to 1835 and 1841 to 1846

Henry "Hank" Aaron (1934) American baseball player who broke Babe Ruth's career home-run record

6

Babe Ruth (1895) American baseball player and first great home run hitter

Ronald Reagan (1911) 40th president of the United States

Mary Leakey (1913) British archaeologist

8

William Sherman (1820) Union Army general in the Civil War

Jules Verne (1828) French author who wrote *Twenty Thousand Leagues Under the Sea*

John Williams (1932) American composer of *Star Wars* film score

9

William H. Harrison (1773) 9th president of the United States

Charles Kingsford Smith (1897) Australian pilot; first to fly across the Pacific with crew

Alice Walker (1944) American author who wrote *The Color Purple*

10

Bertolt Brecht (1898) German writer of plays who wrote *The Good Person of Setzuan*

Elaine Konigsburg (1930) American author who wrote *From the Mixed-Up Files of Mrs. Basil E. Frankweiler*

11

Thomas A. Edison (1847) American inventor of the light bulb

Sir Vivian Fuchs (1908) British scientist and Antarctic explorer

16

Henry Adams (1838) American historian and writer

Hugo Marie De Vries (1848) Dutch plant scientist who worked with heredity

17

Montgomery Ward (1844) American mail-order merchant

Marian Anderson (1897) American singer

Michael Jordan (1963) American basketball star

15

17

22

George Washington (1732) 1st president of the United States

Robert Baden-Powell (1857) British soldier who founded the Boy Scouts in Britain in 1907

23

Sieur de Bienville (1680) French-Canadian explorer and founder of New Orleans

George Frideric Handel (1685) German-born composer

W. E. B. Du Bois (1868) American protest leader and historian

24

Wilhelm Grimm (1786) German collector of fairy tales

Winslow Homer (1836) American painter

Bettino Craxi (1934) Italian prime minister from 1983 to 1987

25

Pierre Auguste Renoir (1841) French impressionist painter

Enrico Caruso (1873) Italian opera singer

George Harrison (1943) British musician who was one of the Beatles

27

Henry Wadsworth Longfellow (1807) American poet who wrote "The Song of Hiawatha"

Rudolf Steiner (1861) Austrian-born philosopher and educator

28

Sir John Tenniel (1820) British cartoonist; illustrator of *Alice's Adventures in Wonderland*

Vaslav Nijinsky (1890) Russian ballet dancer

Linus Pauling (1901) American chemist who won two Nobel Prizes

29

Marquis de Montcalm (1712) French general; died defending Quebec

Gioacchino Antonio Rossini (1792) Italian opera composer who wrote *The Barber of Seville*

Chinese New Year

Firecrackers pop and crackle! Cymbals crash! Drums roll! A giant dragon comes zigzagging down the street decorated with hundreds of sparkling sequins.

Chinese people are celebrating the start of the new year. Friends and family get together for meals. Adults give children little red envelopes with lucky money. And a colorful parade marks the end of several days of festivities.

The Chinese New Year begins on the date of the first new moon between January 21 and February 19. This is because the ancient Chinese calendar is based on the moon. Chinese people around the world observe the holiday. Vietnamese and Koreans also celebrate the new year at this time.

Floating holiday

TRY THIS! **1**

What Chinese year were you born in?

1993 Rooster
1994 Dog
1995 Pig
1996 Rat
1997 Ox
1998 Tiger
1999 Hare
2000 Dragon
2001 Snake
2002 Horse
2003 Sheep
2004 Monkey

Subtract or add 12 from the years listed above to find out what other Chinese years are. For example, 2000 - 12 = 1988, so 1988 was the Year of the Dragon.

Waitangi Day

Hundreds of years ago, people called **Maori** (MAH oh ree) sailed their long canoes to what is now New Zealand. The Maori came from islands in the Pacific.

Hundreds of years later, Europeans came to New Zealand. They brought guns, which increased warfare among the Maori. They also brought diseases that killed thousands of Maori.

The British settlers and the Maori finally got together at a place named Waitangi (why TAHNG ee) to resolve their problems. On February 6, 1840, they signed the Treaty of Waitangi. This agreement made New Zealand a British colony. New Zealand now is an independent nation. It celebrates February 6 as Waitangi Day, its birthday and most important national holiday.

The name *Waitangi* means "Weeping Waters."

KNOW It All!

Valentine's Day

How do you tell your friends and family that you love them? Do you ever send them a valentine?

Many people around the world send valentines on February 14. That's Valentine's Day. On this day, children in the United States, United Kingdom, and Canada often exchange valentine cards with friends. In Italy, people hold a Valentine's Day feast. Wherever Valentine's Day is celebrated, the day gives people a chance to show their love or affection for others.

KNOW It All!!

Valentine's Day is named after Saint Valentine, a Roman Catholic priest who is believed to have been killed for his faith during the middle of the A.D. 200's in Rome. The Roman Catholic Church honors his memory on February 14. Nobody is sure how St. Valentine's name became linked with sending love letters. One English tradition suggests it was because people once believed that birds choose their mates in mid-February.

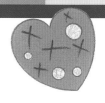

You Will Need:

crayons or markers or colored pencils

construction paper or old magazines

glue

a cup or small can

a clothes hanger

child-safety scissors

string

a thumbtack or pushpin

newspaper

Make Your Own Valentine's Day Mobile

How about making a Valentine's Day mobile?

What To Do:

1. Decide what sizes and colors you want the hearts in your mobile to be. To make a mobile for another holiday, you might use stars for New Year's Eve or a birthday, clovers for St. Patrick's Day, or ghosts and witch hats for Halloween.

2. Draw four or five of the shapes on your construction paper. Your shapes can be all the same size or different sizes. You can use a cup or a can to help you draw a circle.

3. Decorate your shapes using markers or crayons to make festive designs. Or cut out pictures from old magazines and glue them onto the shapes.

4. Cut out your shapes.

5. With a thumbtack, poke holes in the tops of your shapes.

6. Cut different lengths of string for each shape. Thread one end of each string through the holes you made in each shape. Then tie the other end to the clothes hanger.

7. Spread the shapes apart on the hanger until they balance.

8. Hang your finished mobile where everyone can see it.

Don't forget to save your mobile for next year's celebration!

Anniversary of the EDSA Revolution

Do you know what a **revolution** is? It's a big change in government. Many countries have had revolutions. Some countries celebrate the anniversary of revolutions. In the Philippines, people celebrate the anniversary of the EDSA Revolution on February 25.

February
25

On this day in 1986, many **Filipinos** (fihl uh PEE nohz) and leaders of the Roman Catholic Church gathered to demand a change in government. They felt that the government had cheated the people for many years. They wanted a new president.

Some soldiers also wanted a different president. They helped the Filipinos and the Catholic leaders block a main street in Manila called Epifanio de los Santos Avenue (EDSA). The people's protest helped show President Ferdinand Marcos that the people did not want him. So he left the country. This protest became known as the EDSA Revolution.

Every year on the anniversary of the revolution, the leaders of the Roman Catholic Church walk together to the street where the revolution took place. There, they hold a religious ceremony called a Mass to pray for the people of the Philippines and to celebrate the day.

Make Sweet Rice Cakes

One Filipino holiday treat is sweet rice cakes. This recipe makes 8 to 10 rice cakes.

You Will Need:

1 cup (240 ml) white flour
1 teaspoon baking powder
1/2 teaspoon of salt
2 beaten eggs
6 tablespoons coconut milk
1 teaspoon vanilla
1/4 cup (60 ml) sweetened coconut
1 cup (240 ml) boiled white rice
1/2 cup (120 ml) vegetable oil

What To Do:

1. Mix the flour, baking powder, and salt.

2. Add the eggs, coconut milk, coconut, and vanilla to the flour mixture and stir.

3. Add the rice and mix well.

4. Ask a parent for help with the cooking. Heat the oil in a frying pan.

5. Drop large spoonfuls of batter into the oil. Fry the rice cakes until golden brown. Cool slightly, then enjoy plain or with jam.

sweet rice cake

Carnival

Floating holiday

The world's turned topsy-turvy! It's snowing bits of paper. Clowns are dancing with witches. It's the **Mardi Gras** (MAHR dee GRAH) carnival! And people in places as far apart as Venice in Italy and Rio de Janeiro in Brazil are dressing in costumes and masks and dancing and parading in the streets.

Mardi Gras marks the last day of festivities before Lent—40 days of **fasting** and prayer for **Christians** (see page 54). It starts in February or March.

During Mardi Gras, people in Rio de Janeiro, Brazil, dance in the streets.

People also celebrate the days before Lent in other ways. In Britain, people celebrate Pancake Day on the Tuesday before Lent by eating pancakes. The custom began long ago, when people could not eat meat, butter, eggs, and other rich foods during Lent. So, they made pancakes to use up their eggs and butter. In Olney, England, some women have a pancake race. They line up in the market square carrying a pancake in a frying pan. They must flip the pancake three times as they race to the other end of the square.

In Bulgaria, children celebrate Cheese Week before Lent. During the week, the children play a special game. With their hands behind their backs, they try to eat pieces of cheese, eggs, or sweets hanging by a string from the ceiling.

At Mardi Gras in New Orleans, people grab for trinkets that are tossed from parade floats.

Some English women have a pancake race.

Lent

Crowds of people leave the church. A cross of black ashes marks each person's forehead. It's Ash Wednesday, the first day of Lent.

Lent is a Christian religious season. It begins with Ash Wednesday, which falls sometime in February or March. Lent ends about 40 days later on Easter Sunday. The 40 days of Lent remind people of the 40 days Jesus fasted in the wilderness.

Today, many Christians fast by giving up such luxuries as sweets during Lent. They also think about the things they have done wrong in their lives.

In many countries, special foods are eaten during Lent. In Ireland, people have a Lenten dish called champ. It is made of hot mashed potatoes with green onions and served with a lump of butter in the middle.

KNOW It All!

Many religious groups have times of fasting. **Jews** fast on Yom Kippur, the Day of Atonement (see pages 140 and 141). **Muslims** (MUHZ luhmz) fast during the month of Ramadan (see pages 30 and 31).

54

Ash Wednesday is observed in Roman Catholic churches and in some Protestant churches. In Catholic churches, ashes from burned palm leaves are blessed and used to mark a cross on each person's forehead. The ashes remind people that they came from dust and will one day return to dust.

KNOW It All!

These pictures represent some of the famous people born in March. The numbers tell you the days on which they were born. Look at the calendar on the following pages to find out more.

The Month of March

March is the third month of the year. On the Roman calendar, the year began with March. Romans named the month after Mars, their god of war, because they prepared to go off to war in springtime.

In the northern half of the world, people often say that "March comes in like a lion and goes out like a lamb." This means that the weather in early March is often stormy, but by the end, it is mild. In the southern part of the world, March is the beginning of fall.

March

Who Shares My Birthday?

Is your birthday in March? This calendar shows the names of some of the famous people born in March. What do you know about the people who share your birthday?

1

Blanche Kelso Bruce (1841) first full-term African American senator

Harry Belafonte (1927) American singer famous for West Indian songs

Ron Howard (1954) American film director of *Apollo 13*

6

Michelangelo (1475) Italian artist who became one of the most famous artists in history

Elizabeth Barrett Browning (1806) English poet

Valentina Tereshkova (1937) Soviet cosmonaut, first woman in space

7

Kamehameha III (1814) Hawaiian king who gave Hawaii its constitution

Tomás Masaryk (1850) Czech statesman and co-founder of Czechoslovakia

Maurice Ravel (1875) French composer

10

Marcello Malpighi (1628) Italian scientist and pioneer in use of microscope

Kim Campbell (1947) 25th prime minister of Canada; first women to head Canada's government

11

Torquato Tasso (1544) Italian poet

Ezra Jack Keats (1916) American illustrator and author; wrote *The Snowy Day*

Harold Wilson (1916) British prime minister from 1964 to 1970 and 1974 to 1976

12

Sir John J. C. Abbott (1821) 4th prime minister of Canada

Simon Newcomb (1835) American astronomer

Kemal Atatürk (1881) founder and first president of Turkey

13

Joseph Priestley (1733) English chemist who discovered oxygen

Johann Wyss (1781) Swiss author who finished his father's book, *The Swiss Family Robinson*

18

Grover Cleveland (1837) 22nd and 24th president of the United States

Rudolf Diesel (1858) German inventor of the diesel engine

F. W. de Klerk (1936) South African president from 1989 to 1994

19

David Livingstone (1813) British missionary who explored Africa

William Jennings Bryan (1860) American political leader

20

Henrik Ibsen (1828) Norwegian writer of plays

Lois Lowry (1937) American author who wrote *The Giver*

Brian Mulroney (1939) 24th prime minister of Canada

21

Johann Sebastian Bach (1685) German composer

Benito Juárez (1806) Mexican political leader and president

25

Arturo Toscanini (1867) Italian symphony conductor

Elton John (1947) British singer and songwriter

26

Jane Delano (1862) American nurse; organized Red Cross Nursing Service

Fuad I (1868) first king (1922-1936) of independent Egypt

27

Wilhelm Roentgen (1845) German who discovered X rays

Sarah Vaughan (1924) American jazz singer

Mariah Carey (1970) American singer

28

George I (1660) king of England from 1714 to 1727

Pierre Laplace (1749) French astronomer and mathematician

2

Theodor Seuss Giesel (1904) American author and illustrator known as Dr. Seuss; wrote *The Cat in the Hat* and other books

Mikhail Gorbachev (1931) leader of the Soviet Union and Nobel Prize winner in 1990

3

Alexander Graham Bell (1847) American inventor of the telephone

John Murray (1841) Canadian scientist and pioneer in the study of the ocean

4

Antonio Vivaldi (1678) Italian composer

Casimir Pulaski (1747?) Polish patriot; hero of the Revolutionary War

Miriam Makeba (1932) South African singer

5

Gerardus Mercator (1512) Flemish geographer who became the leading mapmaker of the 1500's

Howard Pyle (1853) American writer and illustrator of *The Merry Adventures of Robin Hood* and other children's books

8

Oliver Wendell Holmes, Jr. (1841) American Supreme Court justice for nearly 30 years

Juvenal Habyarimana (1937) Rwandan president (1973-1994) whose death sparked a violent war in Rwanda

9

Amerigo Vespucci (1454) Italian explorer for whom America was named

Samuel Barber (1910) American composer

Yuri A. Gagarin (1934) Soviet cosmonaut and first person to travel in space

14

Johann Strauss, Sr. (1804) Austrian composer known as the "Father of the Waltz"

Albert Einstein (1879) German-born scientist

15

Andrew Jackson (1767) 7th president of the United States

Ruth Bader Ginsburg (1933) American Supreme Court justice and second woman to serve on the Court

16

James Madison (1751) 4th president of the United States

Matthew Flinders (1774) British explorer of Australia

Sid Fleischman (1920) American author who wrote *The Whipping Boy*

17

Kate Greenaway (1846) English illustrator of children's books

Rudolf Nureyev (1938) Soviet-born ballet dancer

22

Randolph Caldecott (1846) English illustrator of children's books

Marcel Marceau (1923) French mime

23

Roger Martin du Gard (1881) French writer and Nobel Prize winner

Akira Kurosawa (1910) Japanese filmmaker who made *The Seven Samurai*

24

John Wesley Powell (1834) American explorer of the Grand Canyon

Harry Houdini (1874) American magician and escape artist

29

29

John Tyler (1790) 10th president of the United States

Pearl Bailey (1918) American singer

Sam Walton (1918) American businessman who founded Wal-Mart

30

Francisco Goya (1746) Spanish painter

Vincent van Gogh (1853) Dutch painter

Celine Dion (1968) Canadian pop singer

31

Joseph Haydn (1732) Austrian composer

Octavio Paz (1914) Mexican poet and philosopher

Cesar Estrada Chávez (1927) Mexican American labor organizer

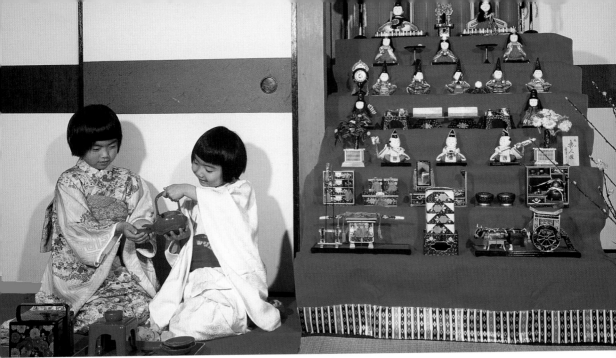

Dolls used in the Girls' Festival represent Japan's **emperor** and empress and members of their court.

Doll Festivals

March 3
May 5

Does your family have special dolls that decorate the shelves or mantel? In Japan, people display special sets of dolls every year on March 3 and May 5. These are doll festival days. The one on March 3 is the Girls' Festival, and the one on May 5 is the Boys' Festival.

During these celebrations, families display dolls that have been handed down for generations. Through the dolls, the children learn about their country's culture, history, and outstanding men and women.

St. Patrick's Day

In Dublin, Ireland, people wear **shamrocks.** In Chicago, the river is dyed green. It's St. Patrick's Day, a good time to wear a bit of green and enjoy Irish **traditions.**

The color green is a reminder of the beautiful green countryside of Ireland. It is also the color of the shamrock, the cloverlike plant that is the national symbol of Ireland.

In Ireland, St. Patrick's Day is a holy day. People attend religious services. Saint Patrick, Ireland's **patron saint**, brought Christianity to Ireland. In many U.S. and Canadian cities, people celebrate with parades and enjoy Irish music and foods. In New York City, more than a hundred bands and a hundred thousand marchers join in the St. Patrick's Day parade along Fifth Avenue. The parade lasts for hours.

Children squirt each other with colored water during the Hindu religious festival called Holi.

Holi

Look out! That splash of red is headed toward you! It's the festival of Holi (HOH lee) in India. The streets are filled with people squirting colored water or smearing brightly colored powder on each other.

Holi is the spring festival that takes place in February and March. It combines singing, dancing, and traditional merrymaking with **Hindu** religious ceremonies. It also reminds Hindus of a story from their mythology.

In the story, a king was angry about his son worshiping Lord Vishnu (VIHSH noo), one of the two main gods of Hinduism. The boy's evil aunt, Holi, tried to kill the boy by taking him into a huge fire. The boy escaped unhurt, but Holi was killed in the fire.

KNOW It All!

Why do the Indians throw colored water and powder on Holi? According to one story, Krishna, a Hindu god, once stole milk from some milkmaids. To get back at him, the milkmaids threw colored powder on him. This custom of throwing colored powder continues on Holi.

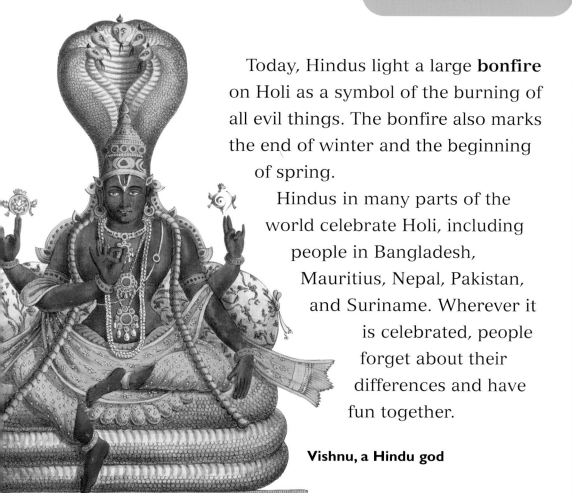

Today, Hindus light a large **bonfire** on Holi as a symbol of the burning of all evil things. The bonfire also marks the end of winter and the beginning of spring.

Hindus in many parts of the world celebrate Holi, including people in Bangladesh, Mauritius, Nepal, Pakistan, and Suriname. Wherever it is celebrated, people forget about their differences and have fun together.

Vishnu, a Hindu god

This colorful sun mask is part of a Moomba Festival parade in the city of Melbourne in Australia.

Moomba

Moomba means "get together and have fun." And that's just what the people of Melbourne, Australia, do at the yearly Moomba Festival.

The Moomba Festival gets its name from the language of the Aborigines, the people who were the first to live in Australia. The festival runs for 11 days. And there is something for everyone.

Among the many events are water shows and boat races on the Yarra River, which flows through the city. At Melbourne Cricket Ground, children's teams play all kinds of sports. There are games of cricket, which is a favorite sport in Australia, as well as soccer and rugby. Children's plays are put on at an outdoor theater.

This young girl is getting clown makeup for the Moomba Festival.

The busy festival ends with a big parade on Australia's Labor Day, the second Monday in March. Bagpipe bands play lively marches and there are colorful floats. The Moomba King and Queen lead the parade. Everywhere there are clowns and more clowns. Children may also dress up and take part in the parade.

St. Joseph's Day

March
19

Huge statues decorate the streets of Valencia, Spain, on St. Joseph's Day.

In Valencia, Spain, wild figures of colorful animals and people made of paper or wood decorate the streets and squares. There are fireworks, parades, and street dances. Then, around midnight, the city lights up with a fiery blaze as all these figures are burned. It's March 19, St. Joseph's Day in Spain!

Saint Joseph was the husband of Mary, the mother of Jesus. Roman Catholics honor Joseph as a **saint**. Most people in Spain are Roman Catholic, so the day is a big celebration in that country. Roman Catholics in other countries also celebrate St. Joseph's Day.

66

Birthday of Benito Juárez

Benito Juárez (behn EE toh HWAH rehs) was one of the greatest leaders in the history of Mexico. His birthday, March 21, is celebrated as a national holiday.

 March 21

Juárez was a Zapotec (ZAH puh tehk) Indian. In 1861, he was elected president of Mexico.

The following year, the French invaded Mexico. When they captured Mexico City, Juárez fled for his life. Traveling about in his black carriage, he led his country's fight for freedom from French control.

In 1866, the United States forced the French to leave Mexico. Juárez, still traveling in his black carriage, returned to his office in Mexico City.

Greek Independence Day

On March 25, 1821, a group of Greek leaders met in a church. They took a vow—liberty or death! At the same time, another group issued a declaration of independence. Finally, in 1829, after eight long years of war, the Greeks won their freedom from Turkey and became an independent nation.

Today, people in Greece celebrate Independence Day on March 25. Many people fly the Greek flag on this day. In Athens, the capital of Greece, there is a big military parade to celebrate the day. Among the marchers are Greek soldiers called evzones (EHV zohns). These soldiers wear a red cap with a black tassel, a colored vest over a white shirt, a white pleated skirt over white tights, and red shoes with a black pompon at the toe.

KNOW It All!!

Who else celebrates Independence Day in March? The African country of Equatorial Guinea celebrates on March 5. Mauritius, an island country in the Indian Ocean, celebrates on March 12. Tunisia in northern Africa celebrates on March 20, and Bangladesh in southern Asia has its holiday on March 26.

Greek soldiers called evzones march in the Greek Independence Day parade.

These pictures represent some of the famous people born in April. The numbers tell you the days on which they were born. Look at the calendar on the following pages to find out more.

The Month of April

April is the fourth month of the year. The Romans called this month *Aprilis*. The name comes from a Latin word that means "to open."

In the northern part of the world, April usually brings more changes than any other month. The last ice and snow disappear. The grass turns green. The buds of trees, shrubs, and flowers begin to open. Birds are singing and building nests. In the southern part of the world, people enjoy mild fall days.

26   27

April

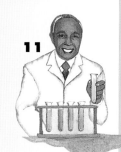

11

Who Shares My Birthday?

Is your birthday in April? This calendar shows the names of some of the famous people born in April. What do you know about the people who share your birthday?

7

1
William Harvey (1578) English doctor; discovered blood circulation

Sergei Rachmaninoff (1873) Russian composer and one of the greatest pianists in history

2
Hans Christian Andersen (1805) Danish writer of fairy tales

Frédéric Bartholdi (1834) French sculptor who designed the Statue of Liberty

10
William Booth (1829) English founder of the Salvation Army

Joseph Pulitzer (1847) American newspaper publisher and creator of Pulitzer Prizes

Clare Boothe Luce (1903) American writer and diplomat

11
Percy Julian (1899) American research chemist

Alberto Ginastera (1916) Argentine composer known for dramatic operas

12
Garcilaso de la Vega (1539) Peruvian historian who wrote about the Inca Empire

Henry Clay (1777) American statesman

Beverly Cleary (1916) American author known for "Henry Huggins" books

13
Thomas Jefferson (1743) 3rd president of the United States

Samuel Beckett (1906) Irish author who won the Nobel Prize in 1969

16
Wilbur Wright (1867) American who invented the airplane with his brother Orville

Kareem Abdul-Jabbar (1947) American basketball star

17
J. P. Morgan (1837) American banker

Nikita Khrushchev (1894) premier of the former Soviet Union

Sirimavo Bandaranaike (1916) Sri Lankan who became world's first female prime minister in 1960

18
Clarence S. Darrow (1857) American criminal lawyer

Leopold Stokowski (1882) English-born orchestra conductor

Hayley Mills (1946) British actress

19
Roger Sherman (1721) only person to sign four documents of American independence

Jean Lee Latham (1902) American author of *Carry On, Mr. Bowditch*

24
Willem de Kooning (1904) Dutch-born painter famous for abstract expressionism

Barbra Streisand (1942) American singer and actress

25
Guglielmo Marconi (1874) Italian inventor of wireless telegraph

Ella Fitzgerald (1917) American jazz singer

Shehu Shagari (1925) Nigerian president from 1979 to 1983

26
John James Audubon (1785) American naturalist and painter

Alfred Krupp (1812) German industrialist

27
Ulysses S. Grant (1822) 18th president of the United States

Ludwig Bemelmans (1898) Austrian-born creator of "Madeline" series

Coretta Scott King (1927) American civil rights leader

2

3

Washington Irving (1783) American author who wrote "Rip Van Winkle"

Jane Goodall (1934) English zoologist noted for her study of chimpanzees

4

Dorothea Dix (1802) American who worked to help the mentally ill and to improve prisons

Maya Angelou (1928) American poet known for her autobiography *I Know Why the Caged Bird Sings*

5

Joseph Lister (1827) English surgeon, first used antiseptic, germ-killing methods in surgery

Booker T. Washington (1856) African American leader and educator

Colin Powell (1937) first African American chair of Joint Chiefs of Staff

6

Raphael (1483) Italian artist of the Renaissance

James Dewey Watson (1928) American biologist; one of the builders of DNA model

7

William Wordsworth (1770) English poet

Gabriela Mistral (1889) Chilean poet; Nobel Prize winner

Jackie Chan (1954) Hong Kong actor of action movies

8

Juan Ponce de León (1474) Spanish explorer

Sonja Henie (1912) Norwegian figure skater; Olympic champion

Trina Schart Hyman (1939) American illustrator of *Saint George and the Dragon*

9

Charles Steinmetz (1865) German-born electrical engineer who did experiments with electric current

Paul Robeson (1898) American actor and singer

16 **23**

14

Christian Huygens (1629) Dutch physicist

Anne Sullivan (1866) American teacher of Helen Keller; writer and champion of the blind

Sir John Gielgud (1904) English actor famous for performances in plays of Shakespeare

15

Nanak (1469) Indian founder of Sikhism, an Indian religion

Leonardo da Vinci (1452) Italian painter, sculptor, and scientist

Henry James (1843) one of America's greatest writers

20

Daniel C. French (1850) American sculptor known for his statue of Abraham Lincoln in the Lincoln Memorial

Joan Miró (1893) Spanish painter

21

Friedrich Fröbel (1782) German founder of kindergarten system

Charlotte Brontë (1816) English author who wrote *Jane Eyre*

Elizabeth II (1926) queen of the United Kingdom

22

Isabella I (1451) Spanish queen who helped Columbus

Madame de Stael (1766) French writer

J. Robert Oppenheimer (1904) American developer of the atomic bomb

23

William Shakespeare (1564) English playwright, considered the greatest dramatist

James Buchanan (1791) 15th president of the United States

Lester B. Pearson (1897) 19th prime minister of Canada

27

28

James Monroe (1758) 5th president of the United States

Charles Stuart (1795) British explorer of Australia

Harper Lee (1926) American author of *To Kill a Mockingbird*

29

Duke Ellington (1899) American jazz composer, pianist, and bandleader

Hirohito (1901) Japanese emperor from 1926 to 1989

30

Mary II (1662) queen of England from 1689 to 1694

Juliana (1909) queen of the Netherlands from 1948 to 1980

April Fools' Day

There's a bug on your shirt!

Did you look to see? If you did—April fool! The joke is on you.

Many people in the United States play tricks on others on April 1. It's April Fools' Day. And on this day, people gleefully shout "April fool" at those they have tricked.

In Scotland, a person who is fooled by being sent on some foolish errand is said to be "hunting the gowk." *Gowk* means "fool."

And in France, a person who is fooled is called a *poisson d'Avril* (PWAHS ahn DAHV rihl), which means "April fish." Why a fish? Perhaps it is because in April fish are young and easily caught. In France, as a special treat, you can buy chocolate fish on April Fools' Day.

KNOW It All!

In France more than 400 years ago, New Year's Day was March 25. Celebrations went through April 1. Then the French adopted a new calendar and New Year's Day changed to January 1. This confused many people for a long time. On April 1, those who remembered the switch began to play tricks on those who forgot.

Buddha's Birthday

Buddha is the title people have given to the **founder** of Buddhism, one of the world's largest religions. The title *Buddha* means "Wise One" or "Enlightened One."

April

8

In Japan, **Buddhists** celebrate his birthday on April 8. On that day in Buddhist temples, children stand in line to approach a tiny, open **shrine** covered with flowers. Inside the shrine is a statue of the baby Buddha. One by one, each child takes a small ladle and pours a little sweet tea over the statue. This is the way the children show their love for Buddha.

This day is also known as the Flower Festival, because it is the time of year when cherry trees begin to blossom.

Buddhists in many other parts of Asia also celebrate Buddha's birthday. In India, people **fast** (by going without food) during the day and pray at home and in temples. In Korea, many people display paper lanterns in the evening. People in Thailand celebrate Buddha's birthday in June.

Make A Snow Leopard Mask

Some Tibetan Buddhists parade and dance with masks to celebrate Buddha's birthday. This snow leopard mask is made of **papier mâché**. Snow leopards are beautiful animals that live in Tibet.

You Will Need:

A paper bag about 12 inches (30 cm) tall that fits loosely over your head

a pencil

scissors

newspaper (lots!)

3 cups (700 milliliters) water

1 cup (235 milliliters) flour

a large mixing bowl

a wooden spoon

gray or white construction paper

gray, white, and black tempera paints

a paintbrush

What To Do:

1. Have an adult help you mark and cut holes in the paper bag for the eyes and nose of your snow leopard.

2. Stuff the paper bag with wadded pages of newspaper. Put it with the open end facing down on several layers of newspaper.

3. To make paste for the papier mâché, stir the water into the flour until the mixture is smooth. Then tear newspaper into strips about 2 inches (5 cm) wide. You will need many strips, some long and some short.

4. Drag a newspaper strip through the paste and glue it flat on the bag. Paste on a layer of newspaper strips in one direction. Then paste another layer of newspaper strips in the other direction. Leave the holes for the eyes and nose uncovered. If the wet bag is hard to work with, let the bag dry between each layer. Cover the bag with four or more layers. Then set the bag on clean newspapers and let it dry at least 24 hours. It may take several days to dry completely.

5. Take the wads of newspaper out of the bag. Paint the bag gray and white. Let the paint dry, then paint black around the eye holes and a black nose and mouth. Add black spots, too.

6. Cut ears for your leopard out of the construction paper. Glue them to the top of the leopard's head. Then have a parade of masks with your friends!

Easter

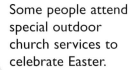

Jesus Christ, the founder of Christianity, died on a cross on a Friday about 2,000 years ago. **Christians** believe that on the following Sunday, Christ arose from the dead and, in so doing, proved that He was the Son of God. The day Jesus died and was buried is known as Good Friday. The following Sunday is Easter.

Christians celebrate Easter by going to church. Some people attend special outdoor services at sunrise. The light of the rising sun reminds them of the light

Some people attend special outdoor church services to celebrate Easter.

that comes back to the world with the newly risen Jesus.

Easter customs include wearing new clothes, which represent new life, and eating lamb, which represents Jesus, "the Lamb of God." Eating and hunting colored Easter eggs are also popular customs. Some children play a game with eggs. They roll the eggs

This beautiful Ukrainian Easter egg was painted by hand.

down a hill. The egg that stays uncracked the longest wins.

Most Christians celebrate Easter on a Sunday between March 22 and April 25. Others celebrate it between April 3 and May 8. Whenever Easter comes, it's the oldest, the most important, and the most joyful of all Christian holy days.

These girls, dressed in their colorful Ukrainian costumes, are dyeing and decorating Easter eggs.

Passover

Long ago, the Jewish people were slaves in Egypt. To help the **Jews**, God told a Jewish man named Moses that he was to lead his people to freedom. God then told Moses what must be done.

Each family was to mark its doorway with the blood of a lamb. The people were to stay in their houses. They were to gather their belongings together and be ready to leave Egypt.

During the night, the Angel of Death visited every Egyptian home. And in each home, the first-born child died. But the Jews were safe. The Angel of Death saw the blood on their doorways and went by, or passed over, their houses. This is how the Jewish feast called Passover got its name.

After this terrible night, the Egyptian king, or pharaoh, let the Jews go. Afraid that the pharaoh might change his mind,

Jews have celebrated Passover for more than 3,000 years. This freedom festival begins on the 15th day of the Hebrew month of Nisan, which is in March or April. It lasts for seven or eight days.

This family is eating matzah, a traditional Passover food.

the Jews hurried out of Egypt. Leaving Egypt, they became free.

Today, Passover begins with the Seder (SAY duhr), which is both a religious service and a feast. The family prays and eats traditional foods. One of these foods is **matzah**, unleavened bread. Traditionally, after the Seder service, everyone sings happy folk songs.

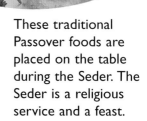

These traditional Passover foods are placed on the table during the Seder. The Seder is a religious service and a feast.

These pictures represent some of the famous people born in May. The numbers tell you the days on which they were born. Look at the calendar on the following pages to find out more.

The Month of May

May is the fifth month of the year. There are several stories about how this month was named. According to one story, May was named for *Maia* (MAY yuh), the Roman goddess of spring and growth.

In parts of the **Northern Hemisphere,** May is one of the most beautiful months of the year. The days are warmer and the flowers are in bloom. In the **Southern Hemisphere,** the days are getting colder.

May

Who Shares My Birthday?

3

Is your birthday in May? This calendar shows the names of some of the famous people born in May. What do you know about the people who share your birthday?

1

Mother (Mary) Jones (1830) labor leader of Appalachian coal miners

M. Scott Carpenter (1925) American astronaut and oceanographer

2

Catherine the Great (1729) German princess who became empress of Russia

Bing Crosby (1904) American singer

Satyajit Ray (1921) Indian film director of international fame

7

Robert Browning (1812) English poet

Johannes Brahms (1833) German composer

Peter Ilich Tchaikovsky (1840) Russian composer

8

Harry S. Truman (1884) 33rd president of the United States

11

Irving Berlin (1888) American songwriter

Martha Graham (1894) American dancer and modern dance choreographer

Salvador Dali (1904) Spanish painter

12

Edward Lear (1812) English artist and author known for light verse

Florence Nightingale (1820) English nurse; founded modern professional nursing

Katharine Hepburn (1907) American actress

17

19

17

Sandro Botticelli (1444) Italian painter

Edward Jenner (1749) English doctor; discovered vaccination against smallpox

Alfonso XIII (1886) king of Spain

18

Nicholas II (1868) last czar of Russia

Dame Margot Fonteyn (1919) British ballerina

Pope John Paul II (1920) Polish-born head of Roman Catholic Church

19

Dame Nellie Melba (1861) Australian opera singer

Malcolm X (1925) American social reformer

Lorraine Hansberry (1930) American playwright who wrote *A Raisin in the Sun*

20

Honoré de Balzac (1799) great French novelist

Antoinette Blackwell (1825) first ordained female American minister

Sigrid Undset (1882) Norwegian author who won a Nobel Prize

25

Ralph Waldo Emerson (1803) American writer

Miles Davis (1926) American jazz trumpeter and bandleader

26

Sally Ride (1951) American astronaut; first American woman in space

John Wayne (1907) American movie actor

27

Isadora Duncan (1877) American dancer and founder of modern dance

Rachel Carson (1907) American biologist who wrote *Silent Spring*

28

Jim Thorpe (1887) American athlete; known as one of the greatest all-around athletes in history

Patrick White (1912) Australian author and Nobel Prize winner

3

Golda Meir (1898) prime minister of Israel from 1969 to 1974

Pete Seeger (1919) American folk singer and composer who wrote "Where Have All the Flowers Gone?"

4

Horace Mann (1796) American educator

Thomas Huxley (1825) English biologist

Audrey Hepburn (1929) Belgian-born film actress; spokesperson for the UN Children's Fund

5

Karl Marx (1818) German philosopher, revolutionary, and writer

Nellie Bly (1867?) American newspaper reporter; her real name was Elizabeth Cochrane

6

Sigmund Freud (1856) Austrian physician who revolutionized ideas on how the mind works

Robert E. Peary (1856) American who discovered the North Pole

Willie Mays (1931) American baseball player; great home run hitter

9

9

John Brown (1800) American antislavery reformer

Sir James Barrie (1860) Scottish author who wrote *Peter Pan*

Howard Carter (1873) English archaeologist who found tomb of Tutankhamen

10

Sir Thomas Johnstone Lipton (1850) Scottish founder of Lipton Tea Company

Fred Astaire (1899) American entertainer

Bono (1960) Irish singer of rock group U2

13

Maria Theresa (1717) Austrian empress

Joe Louis (1914) American boxing champion

Stevie Wonder (1950) American composer, singer, and musician; wrote "You Are the Sunshine of My Life"

14

Gabriel Fahrenheit (1686) German scientist; developed Fahrenheit temperature scale

Robert Owen (1771) Welsh-born social reformer

George Lucas (1944) American filmmaker of *Star Wars*

15

L. Frank Baum (1856) American author of "Oz" books

Pierre Curie (1859) French scientist who, with his wife Marie, discovered radium

16

William Seward (1801) American statesman who purchased Alaska from Russia

Olga Korbut (1956) Soviet Olympic gold medal gymnast

Gabriela Sabatini (1970) Argentinian tennis champion

21

Albrecht Dürer (1471) German artist and scholar

Glenn Hammond Curtiss (1878) American aviator and inventor of aircraft

Malcolm Fraser (1930) prime minister of Australia 1975 to 1983

22

Richard Wagner (1813) German musical composer

Sir Arthur Conan Doyle (1859) British author of stories about Sherlock Holmes

Laurence Olivier (1907) one of the leading English actors of the 1900's

23

Carolus Linnaeus (1707) Swedish botanist who set up a scientific way to name plants and animals

Mary Cassatt (1844) American painter; best known for pictures of mothers and children

24

Victoria (1819) British queen who ruled for 63 years

Jan Christian Smuts (1870) South African statesman who helped form Union of South Africa

Bob Dylan (1941) American musician

27   **28**

29

Patrick Henry (1736) American patriot

John F. Kennedy (1917) 35th president of the United States

30

30

Peter I (1672) Russia's first emperor

Benny Goodman (1909) American clarinetist and bandleader

Rainier III (1923) prince of Monaco

31

Walt Whitman (1819) American poet; wrote *Leaves of Grass*

Elizabeth Coatsworth (1893) American author of books for children

In Canada, Puerto Rico, and the United States, Labor Day falls in September. In Australia, Labor Day is called Eight Hour Day. New Zealanders celebrate Labor Day in October.

KNOW It All!

May Day/ Labor Day

May 1

With flowers in their hair, children dance around a tall pole. They hold colorful ribbons that stream from the top of the pole. As they dance, they weave the ribbons in and out, covering the pole with bright colors. It's May Day in England, and the **Maypole** dance celebrates springtime.

May Day was brought to England by the ancient Romans. In Rome, there was a day in spring when men paraded through the city, carrying a pine tree. There was also a festival to honor Flora, the Roman goddess of springtime. When the Romans conquered England, the pine tree became a Maypole.

On May Day in England, the pole was set up in a village park and decorated with flowers and ribbons. Villagers then danced around the Maypole, much as they do today.

The first of May is also Labor Day in some countries. This holiday honors working people. Many countries celebrate with parades. Many people have a picnic or just relax on this holiday.

87

On Boys' Day in Japan, the largest fish streamer is at the top of the pole. It stands for the oldest son. The shortest streamer is for the youngest son.

Boys' Day/ Children's Day

Does your family hang flags or wind socks outside your home for a decoration? On May 5, many Japanese parents fly carp-shaped kites in honor of their boys. The carp is a fish. It is a symbol of strength, courage, and determination.

May 5 is Boys' Day, Tango no Sekku (tahn goh no sek koo), in Japan. There are many **traditions** on this day. Some families display warrior dolls to remind their sons of hero stories.

In 1948, the Japanese government made this day a double holiday. It started a new national holiday called Children's Day to honor both boys and girls. Other countries also celebrate Children's Day. Some of these countries are Argentina, Iceland, Thailand, and Turkey.

KNOW It All!

A traditional treat of this holiday is a sweet, bean-filled rice cake wrapped and cooked in an oak leaf. The oak symbolizes strength.

Make a Carp Kite

Make your own carp kite and fly it in honor of courage, strength, and determination. The colorful streamers stand for freedom in life.

You Will Need:

paints

a paintbrush

a large paper bag

scissors

lightweight cardboard

a nail

3 pieces of string, each 12 inches (30 cm) long

glue

clear tape

streamers (assorted colors and lengths)

crepe paper

kite string

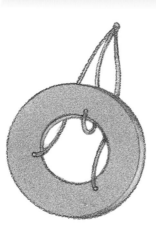

What To Do:

1. Paint a carp lengthwise on the paper bag. The carp mouth should be at the bottom of the bag.

2. Cut out a cardboard ring no bigger than the base of the paper bag. Use the nail to punch three holes on the inside of the ring at different places and evenly spaced.

3. Tie the three pieces of string to the ring holes. Tie the loose ends of the string together.

4. Trace the inside circle of the ring in the center of the bottom of the paper bag. Ask an adult to help you cut out the circle. Glue the ring inside the bag around the hole, with the strings hanging out of the bag.

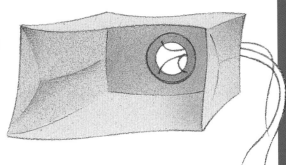

5. Tape streamers to the inside open end of the bag. Tie a long kite string to the knotted end of the three short strings. Now it's time to fly your fish!

To make a truly traditional kite, attach your kite to a stick and place a pinwheel at the top of the stick. Put the stick in a flag holder on your porch or parade your kite down your block.

Victoria Day

On the Monday before May 25, Canadians celebrate the birthdays of two British queens born more than 100 years apart. The first queen was Queen Victoria. She was born on May 24, 1819. British people celebrated her birthday every year. After Queen Victoria's death, Canadians continued to celebrate her birthday to express their loyalty to the British Empire. The holiday is named in her honor.

The second queen is the current British queen, Queen Elizabeth II. She was born on April 21, 1926, but Canadians celebrate her birthday on Victoria Day.

KNOW It All!

Many other countries also celebrate the birthdays of queens and kings. The people of the Netherlands celebrate Queen's Day on April 30.

The Festival of Sacrifice

Colored lights line the village streets. Children play all day in their best clothing, and friends exchange gifts. It's the Festival of Sacrifice. **Muslims** (MUHZ luhmz) in Egypt and other countries are celebrating.

The Festival of Sacrifice takes place at different times. But it always happens at the end of the **hajj**, or annual journey to Mecca. Once in their lifetime, all Muslims are required to make this journey, called a **pilgrimage**, if they are able.

Mecca is the holiest city of Islam, the religion of the Muslims. It lies in western Saudi Arabia. The city is the birthplace of Muhammad, the **prophet** of Islam.

During the festival, animals are also sacrificed in memory of Abraham, a prophet in the Bible. Abraham prevented the sacrifice of his son through his faithfulness to God.

These lights are hanging over the Damascus gate in Syria during the Festival of Sacrifice.

Mother's Day

Floating holiday

How do you show your mother that you love her? Do you like to share stories with her? Do you do favors for her? Do you like to draw pictures for her?

All over the world, people honor mothers and grandmothers in many ways. But in the United States, Canada, and Australia, a special day is set aside just to honor mothers. It is Mother's Day, and it falls on the second Sunday in May.

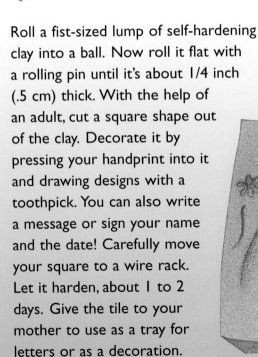

Roll a fist-sized lump of self-hardening clay into a ball. Now roll it flat with a rolling pin until it's about 1/4 inch (.5 cm) thick. With the help of an adult, cut a square shape out of the clay. Decorate it by pressing your handprint into it and drawing designs with a toothpick. You can also write a message or sign your name and the date! Carefully move your square to a wire rack. Let it harden, about 1 to 2 days. Give the tile to your mother to use as a tray for letters or as a decoration.

TRY THIS! 2

On this special day, some children make cards and gifts for their mothers and grandmothers. Other countries of the world also have special days for mothers. For example, people of Malawi celebrate Mother's Day on October 17. In Spain, mothers are honored on December 8.

KNOW It All!

What about fathers? Do they have a special day, too? Of course, they do. Read about Father's Day on pages 104 and 105.

95

These pictures represent some of the famous people born in June. The numbers tell you the days on which they were born. Look at the calendar on the following pages to find out more.

The Month of June

June is the sixth month of the year. Some people say that June was named for *Juno* (JOO noh), the Roman goddess of marriage. Others think that the name came from the Latin word *juniores*, meaning "young men." These people say that the Romans held June sacred to young men, just as they held May sacred to the *majores*, or "older men."

In the northern half of the world, summer begins on June 20, 21, or 22. In the southern part of the world, this is when winter starts.

12

June

Who Shares My Birthday?

3

Is your birthday in June? This calendar shows the names of some of the famous people born in June. What do you know about the people who share your birthday?

1

Jacques Marquette (1637) French explorer known for exploration of Mississippi River in the U.S.A.

Brigham Young (1801) American who led the Mormons from Illinois to Utah

2

John Randolph of Roanoke (1773) American statesman

Thomas Hardy (1840) English author of *Tess of the d'Urbervilles*

Sir Edward W. Elgar (1857) British composer; known for "Pomp and Circumstance"

7

Paul Gauguin (1848) French artist

Gwendolyn Brooks (1917) American poet; winner of a Pulitzer Prize

John N. Turner (1929) 23rd prime minister of Canada

8

Robert Stevenson (1772) Scottish inventor of flashing light in lighthouses

Frank Lloyd Wright (1867) American architect; one of America's most influential architects

13

13

William Butler Yeats (1865) Irish poet

Carlos Chávez (1899) Mexican composer

Christo (1935) Bulgarian-born artist; known for wrapping huge objects such as Pont Neuf, Paris's oldest bridge

14

Harriet Beecher Stowe (1811) American author of *Uncle Tom's Cabin*

Bruce Degen (1945) American illustrator of "The Magic School Bus" series

Steffi Graff (1969) German tennis champion

15

Edward, the Black Prince (1330) one of the most famous English warriors in history

Edvard Grieg (1843) Norwegian composer

Helen Hunt (1963) American TV and movie actress

20

Alberto Santos-Dumont (1873) Brazilian aviator and airplane builder

Lillian Hellman (1905) American writer of plays

John Goodman (1952) American television and film actor

21

Daniel C. Beard (1850) founder of the Boy Scouts of America

Benazir Bhutto (1953) prime minister of Pakistan from 1988 to 1990 and 1993 to 1996

Prince William (1982) British prince in line to the throne

20   21

26

Sir Robert L. Borden (1854) 9th and 10th prime minister of Canada

Babe Didrikson Zaharias (1911?) American athlete; one of greatest in history

27

Charles Parnell (1846) Irish patriot who helped Ireland obtain self-government

Helen Keller (1880) famous deaf and blind American speaker and author

28

Henry VIII (1491) king of England who separated Church of England from Roman Catholic Church

Peter Paul Rubens (1577) Flemish painter

29

George Goethals (1858) American engineer who built the Panama Canal

Antoine de Saint-Exupery (1900) French pilot best known for his book *The Little Prince*

3

Jefferson Davis (1808) president of the Confederate States of America

George V (1865) king of Great Britain during World War I

Charles R. Drew (1904) American doctor; set up blood banks

4

George III (1738) king of Great Britain from 1760 to 1820

Alla Nazimova (1879) Russian actress; famous for her work in U.S. films and stage plays

5

Adam Smith (1723) Scottish economist who wrote *The Wealth of Nations*

John Couch Adams (1819) British astronomer who discovered Neptune

Charles Joseph Clark (1939) 21st prime minister of Canada

6

Nathan Hale (1755) American patriot hanged as a spy by the British

Thomas Mann (1875) German author who won a Nobel Prize

Cynthia Rylant (1954) American author of "Henry and Mudge" series

9

George Stephenson (1781) English inventor; known as "Founder of Railways"

Baroness Bertha von Suttner (1843) Austrian woman who worked for peace, 1905 Nobel Peace Prize winner

10

Prince Philip (1921) Duke of Edinburgh; husband of Queen Elizabeth II

Maurice Sendak (1928) American illustrator and author who wrote *Where the Wild Things Are*

11

Jeanette Rankin (1880) first woman member of U.S. Congress

Jacques-Yves Cousteau (1910) French marine explorer

Robert Munsch (1945) American-born author of *Thomas' Snowsuit*

12

Johanna Spyri (1827) Swiss author of *Heidi*

George Bush (1924) 41st president of the United States

Anne Frank (1929) German-Jewish girl; famous for the diary she kept while hiding from the Nazis

16

Arthur Meighen (1874) 11th and 13th prime minister of Canada

Katharine Graham (1917) American newspaper publisher of *The Washington Post*

17

Charles Gounod (1818) French composer of operas

Igor Stravinsky (1882) Russian-born composer; famous for his ballet music

18

Paul McCartney (1942) English rock star; one of the Beatles

Chris Van Allsburg (1949) American author and illustrator who wrote *The Polar Express*

19

Blaise Pascal (1623) French philosopher, mathematician, and scientist

Aung San Suu Kyi (1945) Burmese political leader, human rights activist, and Nobel Prize winner

22

Julian Huxley (1887) English biologist

Katherine Dunham (1912) American dancer and choreographer whose work was influenced by Caribbean culture

23

Josephine (1763) empress of France and wife of Napoleon Bonaparte

Edward VIII (1894) English king who gave up his throne to marry Wallis Simpson

24

E. I. du Pont (1771) French-born founder of one of the world's largest chemical companies

Jean Marzollo (1942) American author of "Punch and Play" storybooks

25

Louis Mountbatten (1900) British admiral and World War II hero

Celia Franca (1921) British ballet dancer; directed National Ballet of Canada

Eric Carle (1929) American author and illustrator

30

Stanley Spencer (1891) English artist

Czeslaw Milosz (1919) Polish-born writer and Nobel Prize winner

26

22

27

Dragon Boat Festival

Gongs, drums,
and horns urge rowers in
racing boats to go faster.
The rowers in each boat follow the
rhythm of their drummer. As the drums
beat faster, the boats skim over the
water like racing dragons in honor of
a poet who died long ago.

The poet was Qu Yuan (choo yoo ahn).
More than 2,000 years ago, Qu Yuan fell
into a river. When people saw what had
happened, they put their boats into the

water and raced to rescue him. But his body was never found. Ever since Qu Yuan disappeared, the Chinese have remembered the race to find him with the Dragon Boat Festival.

The big event of the festival is a colorful boat race. Each boat is painted like a dragon.

Chinese people throughout Asia and in other parts of the world enjoy the Dragon Boat Festival every summer. This celebration comes in the month of the fifth moon on the Chinese calendar— between May 28 and June 28.

Shavuot—Day of the Commandments

Shavuot (sha VOO oht) is one of the great Jewish festivals. Jewish people celebrate it as the day that God gave the Ten Commandments to Moses, the Jewish leader.

Shavuot is the Hebrew word for "weeks." This festival is also called Feast of Weeks because it comes seven weeks after the first day of Passover (see pages 80 and 81).

During the bar mitzvah ceremony, a Jewish boy reads a passage from the Torah in Hebrew.

Long ago, Shavuot was also a harvest festival. It was the time when **Jews** made a journey to Jerusalem to make offerings at the Temple in thanks for their crops. After the Romans destroyed the Temple, Shavuot became a time to celebrate the gift of the Ten Commandments.

Today, Shavuot is when some Jews celebrate the confirmation of children. Jewish boys are confirmed when they reach the age of 13. Girls are confirmed at the age of 12. The ceremony of confirmation is called **bar mitzvah** (bahr MIHTS vuh) for boys and **bat mitzvah** (baht MIHTS vuh) for girls. The name means son (or daughter) of the commandment.

Jews living in the city of Jerusalem celebrate Shavuot at a holy place called the Wailing Wall. The decorated covering protects a large scroll on which the Torah (the first five books of the Bible) is written.

Father's Day

People all over the world find different ways to show fathers their love and respect. Father's Day is a special day set aside to honor fathers.

In some countries, children make gifts for their fathers for Father's Day. Many people send cards that express their love. People also like to take their fathers to shows or sports events they enjoy on that day. Sometimes on Father's Day, children help out their fathers in special ways, such as by doing extra chores.

Children in Serbia, a country in Eastern Europe, tease their dads on Father's Day. They tie him in bed and tease him until they get coins and treats.

Grandfathers are honored on Father's Day, too. Many people make a point to visit their grandfathers on this day.

Father's Day is celebrated in June in the United States, Canada, and England. People in Australia honor their fathers during September. In Serbia, people celebrate Father's Day on the Sunday before Christmas.

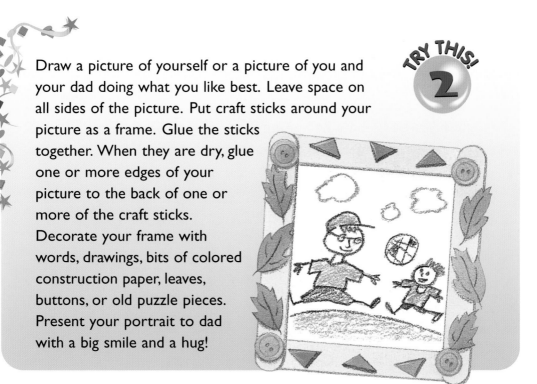

Draw a picture of yourself or a picture of you and your dad doing what you like best. Leave space on all sides of the picture. Put craft sticks around your picture as a frame. Glue the sticks together. When they are dry, glue one or more edges of your picture to the back of one or more of the craft sticks. Decorate your frame with words, drawings, bits of colored construction paper, leaves, buttons, or old puzzle pieces. Present your portrait to dad with a big smile and a hug!

TRY THIS!
2

June 6

Flag Day

On Flag Day in Sweden, June 6, the Swedes honor the day in 1523 when Gustavus I (guh STAY vuhs) became king and Sweden became an independent country. Before then, Sweden was part of a group of countries ruled by the king and queen of Denmark. Sweden was part of this group for many years. But some people were not happy under Danish rulers. Gustavus was one of them. He joined the fight for independence from Denmark when he was 18 years old. Sweden won its

Spread out newspapers to protect your table. Cut out a piece of cotton cloth 8 x 10 inches (20 x 25 cm). Ask an adult to help you glue the end of the flag around a rod about 2 feet (60 cm) long. Let the glue dry. Now you have a flag on a flagpole.

Use a pencil to draw a design or picture on one side of your flag. Then paint your design with watercolors. The paint will soak through to show on both sides of the cloth. Let the paint dry. Wave your flag proudly on Flag Day—or any day!

TRY THIS! 2

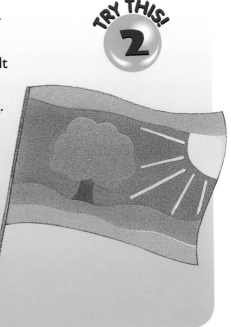

These children in Sweden are celebrating Flag Day with homemade flags.

independence, and the happy Swedes elected Gustavus as their king.

Today, Swedes celebrate the day with parades. Many people fly the country's flag outside their home. The king and queen of Sweden also give flags to schools, sports clubs, and other groups in a special ceremony.

There are other flag days in June. The United States celebrates Flag Day on June 14. Finland's flag day is the Saturday closest to June 24.

Midsummer Day

Long ago, people in Europe worshiped the sun. So the return of summer was a time of great rejoicing. The people lit **bonfires**—symbols of the sun—and celebrated all night and into the next day.

This time was known as Midsummer Eve (June 23) and Midsummer Day (June 24). This, of course, is not midsummer. In the **Northern Hemisphere,** summer begins on June 20, 21, or 22, when the sun is at its highest point in the sky.

Years ago, the early **Christian** Church chose Midsummer Day as the birthdate of John the Baptist, who is a great Christian **saint**.

People in many Christian countries have celebrated St. John's Day for hundreds of years. These celebrations are a curious mixture of old and new customs. There are bonfires, but these are now called St. John's Fire. And, of course, there is a great deal of merrymaking.

KNOW It All!

Baptism is a religious ceremony involving water. Saint John was called John the Baptist because he baptized people, including Jesus. Baptism marks a person's entry into the Christian faith.

TRY THIS!
1

We appreciate the sun for many reasons. Can you list five reasons why the sun is important to us?

American Indians in New Mexico dance a corn dance in celebration of St. John's Day.

These pictures represent some of the famous people born in July. The numbers tell you the days on which they were born. Look at the calendar on the following pages to find out more.

The Month of July

July is the seventh month of the year. The Romans named this month *Julius*, in honor of Julius Caesar.

In most countries in the **Northern Hemisphere**, July is usually the hottest month of the year. In the **Southern Hemisphere**, July is one of the winter months. Except for cold Antarctica and the cold rainy part of South America, the climate during July is mild in most countries in the Southern Hemisphere.

12

30

18

July

Who Shares My Birthday?

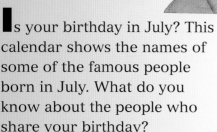

6

Is your birthday in July? This calendar shows the names of some of the famous people born in July. What do you know about the people who share your birthday?

1

Comte de Rochambeau (1725) French general who fought in the Revolutionary War

George Sand (1804) French writer

Carl Lewis (1961) American Olympic champion

2

Sir Charles Tupper (1821) 7th prime minister of Canada

Olav V (1903) king of Norway from 1957 to 1991

Thurgood Marshall (1908) first black justice of the U.S. Supreme Court

7

Marc Chagall (1887) Russian-born artist

Gian Carlo Menotti (1911) American opera composer who wrote *Amahl and the Night Visitors*

Ringo Starr (1940) English drummer with the Beatles

8

Jean de la Fontaine (1621) French author of fables

Ferdinand von Zeppelin (1838) German inventor of airships

Raffi (1948) Armenian-Canadian singer and songwriter

11

Robert I (1274) Scottish king who freed Scotland from England

John Quincy Adams (1767) 6th president of the United States

E. B. White (1899) American author of *Charlotte's Web*

12

Julius Caesar (100? B.C.) Roman military leader and statesman

Pablo Neruda (1904) Chilean poet and Nobel Prize winner

Bill Cosby (1937) American entertainer

13

Mary Emma Woolley (1863) American educator; active in world peace movements

Marcia Brown (1918) American illustrator known for *Shadow*

Wole Soyinka (1934) Nigerian author and Nobel Prize winner

14

James Abbott McNeil Whistler (1834) American painter

Woody Guthrie (1912) American folksinger

Gerald R. Ford (1913) 38th president of the United States

19

Samuel Colt (1814) American who developed a pistol named after him

Edgar Degas (1834) French impressionist painter who is known for scenes of ballet dancers

20

Petrarch (1304) Italian poet and scholar

Sir Edmund Hillary (1919) New Zealander; one of the first two men to reach the top of Mount Everest

Paulette Bourgeois (1951) Canadian author of *Franklin in the Dark*

19

18

20

25

Thomas Eakins (1844) one of greatest American realist painters of 1800's

Elias Canetti (1905) Bulgarian author and Nobel Prize winner

26

George Bernard Shaw (1856) Irish-born playwright

Carl Jung (1875) Swiss psychologist

Jan Berenstain (1923) American creator of "Berenstain Bears" series

27

Alexandre Dumas (1824) French author

Peggy Fleming (1948) American Olympic skating champion

28

Beatrix Potter (1866) British author and illustrator of *The Tale of Peter Rabbit* and other children's books

Marcel Duchamp (1887) French-born painter and a pioneer of Dada art

3

Richard B. Bennett (1870) 15th prime minister of Canada

Franz Kafka (1883) Czech author of short stories and novels

Tom Stoppard (1937) English playwright

4

Calvin Coolidge (1872) 30th president of the United States

King Taufa'ahau Toupou IV (1918) king of Tonga when it became independent in 1970

5

David G. Farragut (1801) first admiral of the U.S. Navy

P. T. Barnum (1810) American showman; famous for his circus

Cecil Rhodes (1853) British businessman and statesman; expanded British Empire in Africa

6

John Paul Jones (1747) American naval hero; famous for saying "I have not yet begun to fight!"

14th Dalai Lama (1935) Tibetan religious and political leader; winner of 1989 Nobel Peace Prize

8

15

9

Elias Howe (1819) American inventor of the first practical sewing machine

Tom Hanks (1956) American actor who starred in *Forrest Gump* and *Apollo 13*

10

Mary Bethune (1875) American educator who worked to improve educational opportunities for African Americans

Arthur Ashe (1943) American tennis star

15

Inigo Jones (1573) major English architect

Rembrandt van Rijn (1606) Dutch painter; the Netherlands' greatest artist

Maria Cabrini (1850) first U.S. citizen to be made a Roman Catholic saint

16

Mary Baker Eddy (1821) American founder of Christian Science

Roald Amundsen (1872) Norwegian explorer; led first expedition to South Pole

17

Isaac Watts (1674) English preacher and hymn writer who is known for "Joy to the World"

John Jacob Astor (1763) German-born fur trader

18

Nelson Mandela (1918) president of South Africa; became the country's first black president

John Glenn (1921) first American astronaut to orbit the earth

21

Ernest Hemingway (1899) American author and Nobel Prize winner

Isaac Stern (1920) American violinist; debuted with the San Francisco Orchestra at age 11

22

Gregor Mendel (1822) Austrian botanist and monk who discovered rules of heredity

Stephen Vincent Benét (1898) American poet who wrote *John Brown's Body*

23

Arthur W. Brown (1886) British aviator who made the first transatlantic flight in 1919

Raymond Chandler (1888) American author of detective stories

24

Simón Bolivar (1783) Venezuelan general who helped five South American nations win independence

Amelia Earhart (1897) American aviator; first woman to fly across the Atlantic Ocean alone

24

28

31

29

William Beebe (1877) American naturalist and writer who became famous for his stories of undersea exploration

30

Emily Brontë (1818) British author who wrote *Wuthering Heights*

Henry Ford (1863) American who founded Ford Motor Company

31

John Ericsson (1803) Swedish-American inventor

Evonne Goolagong Cawley (1951) Australian tennis star

Canada Day

July 1

Canada has a birthday on July 1. It's Canada Day. People across Canada celebrate this national holiday with parades, fireworks, and other festivities.

Canada was once part of Great Britain. In time, it formed its own government. This new nation remained loyal to Britain.

On July 1, 1867, the British government approved the plan to make Canada an independent country. It was called the Dominion of Canada. The new country had only 4 provinces. Now Canada has 10 provinces and 3 territories.

Canada no longer calls itself a dominion, so July 1 is now Canada Day instead of its former name, Dominion Day.

The Police Pipe Band adds to the excitement of Canada Day in Vancouver, British Columbia.

Scottish dancing is one of the many contests held at the Highland Games.

Highland Games

Bagpipes sound and drums thunder. Men and women in tartan **kilts** perform traditional Scottish dances. All around are contests of athletics and strength. It's the Highland Games, traditional Scottish contests of athletics, dancing, and music.

There are races, jumping contests, and more. One of the unusual events at the games is the caber-throwing contest. A caber looks a bit like a short telephone pole. This game is a test of strength.

Highland games were first held in the rugged Highlands of northern Scotland. Today, they are held at different times in Scotland, Canada, New Zealand, and the United States.

Tossing the caber takes a lot of strength.

Independence Day

On July 4, 1776, American leaders got together and declared their freedom from England. They gave their reasons on a famous paper called the Declaration of Independence. This important paper said the people had the right to be free.

The Revolutionary War was going on at the time. It was the American colonists' fight for freedom from England. Finally, in 1783, peace and independence came to the patriots, and the United States of America was born.

Today, people in the United States celebrate the Fourth of July with parades, picnics, fireworks, and other festivities.

KNOW It All!

Many countries around the world celebrate the day they won their independence. To find out how some other countries won their independence and how they celebrate it, look up the pages listed under "Independence Day" in the index.

These girls are putting lanterns in the river for Bon, which is also known as the Festival of Lanterns.

Bon Festival

The smell of **incense** fills the air. Paper lanterns light up homes and **cemeteries**. It's the Japanese festival of Bon, the time of year when **Buddhists** believe the spirits of their **ancestors** come to visit them. The festival takes place from July 13 to 15.

During the festival, Buddhists light paper lanterns at their homes to guide the spirits. They also leave food in their homes and cemeteries to welcome the spirits. Families go to the cemetery to clean family graves. They may also entertain guests at home or exchange gifts.

On the last evening, families float the lanterns down rivers or on the sea. They believe the lanterns carry the spirits back to the spirit world.

117

Bastille Day

In Paris, France, on July 14, 1789, a ragged mob of people swept through the streets shouting for justice. The people were on their way to the Bastille (bas TEEL), a dreadful prison.

The Bastille stood for all that was evil in France. At that time, the king and the rich lived in luxury. The poor were often starving and treated badly. Anyone who complained was thrown into a prison such as the Bastille.

But on that day in July, the people rose up in anger. They stormed the Bastille, freed the prisoners, and began to tear down the prison. This event was part of the French Revolution. The **revolution** led to greater freedom and a better government for the French people.

Today, French people everywhere celebrate July 14 in memory of that important day in 1789. It is Bastille Day, a national holiday in France.

The celebration of Bastille Day includes parades, games, speeches, and fireworks. In the evening, people dance in the street until dawn, just as they did on the first Bastille Day.

The exciting Bastille Day parade passes through the Arc de Triomphe (Arch of Triumph) in Paris.

Bastille Day ice cream

Bring the colors of the French flag to your table with Bastille Day ice cream.

You Will Need:

a half gallon (2 liters) of white vanilla ice cream

a sturdy spoon

a mixing bowl

red and blue food coloring (use paste coloring for darker colors)

a large bread pan

a spatula

plastic wrap

a knife

What To Do:

1. Scoop out one third of the ice cream. Soften it in the bowl for 10 minutes.

2. Stir blue food coloring into the ice cream. Spread the blue ice cream over the bottom of the bread pan and freeze for 30 minutes. Wash your bowl and spoon.

3. Scoop out another third of the ice cream. Let it soften for 10 minutes. Then spread a layer of white ice cream over the blue ice cream. Freeze for 30 minutes.

4. Scoop out the remaining ice cream. Let it soften for 10 minutes. Add red food coloring and stir. Spread the red ice cream over the white layer.

5. Cover the pan with plastic wrap and freeze for several hours.

6. Dip the bottom of the pan in warm water for a few seconds to loosen the ice cream. Then use a wet knife to cut slices of the ice cream. Enjoy!

Simón Bolívar's Birthday

July
24

Simón Bolívar is one of the greatest heroes of South America. He was born in Venezuela in 1783 and became a general for a South American army. Bolívar fought for the freedom of the Spanish colonies in South America.

In 1819, Bolívar became the first president of a union of South American countries. Finally, in 1824, Bolívar crushed the Spanish army. He had won independence for what are now Bolivia, Colombia, Ecuador, Panama, Peru, and Venezuela.

Those six countries honor Simón Bolívar on his birthday, July 24.

The country of Bolivia was named in Bolívar's honor, and a silver coin used today in Venezuela is called the *bolívar*.

These pictures represent some of
the famous people born in August.
The numbers tell you the days on
which they were born. Look at the
calendar on the following pages to
find out more.

The Month of August

August is the eighth month of the year. After Julius Caesar was killed, Augustus, his great-nephew, became **emperor** of Rome. The Romans named August in his honor.

In parts of the **Northern Hemisphere**, August is summertime. It is likely to be one of the hottest months there. In the **Southern Hemisphere**, the arrival of August means that winter will soon be over.

18

4

16

August

24

Who Shares My Birthday?

Is your birthday in August? This calendar shows the names of some of the famous people born in August. What do you know about the people who share your birthday?

1
Francis Scott Key (1779) American who wrote "The Star-Spangled Banner"

Maria Mitchell (1818) American astronomer

Herman Melville (1819) American author who wrote *Moby-Dick*

2
John Tyndall (1820) British physicist

James Baldwin (1924) American author who wrote *Go Tell It on the Mountain*

James Howe (1946) American author of "Bunnicula" series

7
Louis Leakey (1903) British scientist who, with wife Mary, found evidence of human origins

Ralph Bunche (1904) American statesman; Nobel Peace Prize winner

8
Nathaniel Brown Palmer (1799) American explorer who may have been the first person to see Antarctica

Marjorie Kinnan Rawlings (1896) American author who wrote *The Yearling*

11
Carrie Jacobs Bond (1862) American writer of popular songs

Alex Haley (1921) American author known for his book *Roots*

Joanna Cole (1944) American author and creator of the "Magic School Bus" series

12
Katharine Lee Bates (1859) American poet who wrote the words to the song "America the Beautiful"

Cecil B. DeMille (1881) American motion-picture producer and director known for Biblical movies

13
Lucy Stone (1818) American women's rights leader

Annie Oakley (1860) American Wild West show performer known for her sharpshooting

14
John Ringling North (1903) American whose family ran the world's largest circus

Gary Larson (1950) American cartoonist known for "The Far Side"

19
Orville Wright (1871) American pioneer, aviator, and airplane designer

Bill Clinton (1946) 42nd president of the United States

20
Oliver Hazard Perry (1785) American naval officer; hero of the Battle of Lake Erie

Benjamin Harrison (1833) 23rd president of the United States

Rajiv Gandhi (1944) prime minister of India from 1984 to 1989

21
Count Basie (1904) American jazz pianist and bandleader

26

18

21

26
Antoine Lavoisier (1743) French chemist

Mother Teresa (1910) Roman Catholic nun who worked with the poor in India; Nobel Peace Prize winner

27
Margaretha Schurz (1833) German-born teacher who established the first U.S. kindergarten

Lyndon B. Johnson (1908) 36th president of the United States

28
Johann van Goethe (1749) German poet, novelist, and playwright who wrote *Faust*

Eliel Saarinen (1873) Finnish architect who helped develop the skyscraper

29
Oliver Wendell Holmes (1809) American author and doctor

Maurice Maeterlinck (1862) Belgian poet and playwright

3
Alfred Deakin (1856) Australian prime minister in early 1900's

P. D. James (1920) English writer known for detective stories

4
Louis Armstrong (1901) American jazz singer and trumpet player

Knut Hamsun (1859) Norwegian author and Nobel Prize winner

Elizabeth, the Queen Mother (1900) wife of George VI of the United Kingdom

5
Edward John Eyre (1815) British explorer; first European to make a major overland crossing of Australia

Neil Armstrong (1930) American astronaut; first person to set foot on the moon

6
Alfred, Lord Tennyson (1809) English poet

Sir Alexander Fleming (1881) Scottish scientist who discovered penicillin

Barbara Cooney (1916) American author and illustrator

9
Izaak Walton (1593) English author; known for book on rural life

John Dryden (1631) English poet and writer of plays

Patricia C. McKissack (1944) American author of "Great African American" series

10
Herbert Hoover (1874) 31st president of the United States

Muhammad V (1909) the first ruler of independent Morocco

Jimmy Dean (1928) American country and western singer

15
Napoleon Bonaparte (1769) emperor of France

Sir Walter Scott (1771) Scottish author of *Ivanhoe*

Princess Anne (1950) daughter of Queen Elizabeth II

16
Gabriel Lippmann (1845) French physicist and Nobel Prize winner

Menachim Begin (1913) Israeli president from 1977 to 1983, Nobel Peace Prize winner

Madonna (1958) American pop singer

17
Davy Crockett (1786) American frontiersman who was killed defending the Alamo

Menelik II (1844) one of the greatest emperors of Ethiopia

Robert DeNiro (1943) American actor

18
Vijaya Lakshmi Pandit (1900) one of India's most famous women, known for work in government

Roberto Clemente (1934) Puerto Rican baseball player; one of greatest in history

22
Claude Debussy (1862) French composer

Sir John Forrest (1847) Australian explorer; first premier of Western Australia

23
Baron Cuvier (1769) French naturalist who began the study of fossils

Edgar Lee Masters (1869) American poet and biographer

Queen Noor (1951) American-born queen of Jordan

24
William Wilberforce (1759) British leader in the fight to get rid of slavery in the British Empire

Yasir Arafat (1929) Palestinian political leader and winner of the Nobel Peace Prize

25
Bret Harte (1836) American author of stories about the West

Leonard Bernstein (1918) American conductor, composer, and pianist

Althea Gibson (1927) American tennis champion

30
Mary Shelley (1797) English author of *Frankenstein*

Ernest Rutherford (1871) British physicist; "father of nuclear science"

31
Maria Montessori (1870) Italian educator

Wilhelmina (1880) queen of the Netherlands during both world wars

Star Festival

Once upon a time, two stars—Vega (VEE guh) and Altair (al TAH ihr)—fell in love. After Vega and Altair married, they neglected their duties. This made Vega's father—the king of the heavens—angry. He sent Altair to live far away in a place known as the Heavenly River. He said the two could see each other only once a year on the seventh day of the seventh moon.

When this day came, poor Vega could not cross the Heavenly River. A flock of magpies took pity on her. They spread their wings to make a bridge, and Vega ran across the bridge to reach Altair.

According to this tale, Vega and Altair continue to meet this way. But if it rains on this day, the magpies cannot make a bridge. Then Vega and Altair must wait another year.

The Japanese people love this story. They call the seventh day of the seventh moon the Star Festival.

People in the city of Sendai, Japan, celebrate this festival from August 6 to 8. They decorate streets and bamboo branches with colorful paper blossoms and figures. These figures are offerings to Vega and Altair and are meant to bring good luck.

Vega and Altair are the names of two bright stars in the sky.

KNOW It All!

Make A Paper Cat

During the Star Festival, some people hang folded paper figures in streets and on tree branches. You can make a paper cat to hang up during the festival. Ask an adult to help you follow the diagram.

You Will Need:

1 square sheet of white or
   colored paper
clear tape
marking pens
10 inches (25 cm) of thread
1 needle

What To Do:

1. Fold the paper in half, corner to corner. Now you have a triangle.

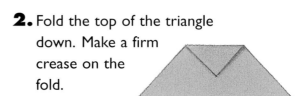

2. Fold the top of the triangle down. Make a firm crease on the fold.

3. Fold the two other corners up, leaving a point at the bottom. They should be folded up to the sides of the crease on top.

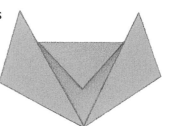

4. Tape the folded sections down. Then, turn the paper over. Draw the face of your cat.

5. Ask an adult to help you thread the needle and poke the needle and thread through the top of the cat. Tie a knot in the string and hang up your paper cat. May you have good luck the rest of your life!

Indonesian Independence Day

August 17

In the city of Jakarta, Indonesia, flags fly everywhere on Independence Day, even on betjaks (BEH chahks). A betjak is a kind of taxi for one or two passengers. It looks like a bicycle with three wheels. The driver pedals from the rear.

As the drivers pedal through the busy streets, clanging their bells as they go, the red and white flag of Indonesia flaps in the breeze in celebration of the country's independence.

Indonesia gained its independence from the Dutch on August 17, 1945. It had been under Dutch rule for 150 years.

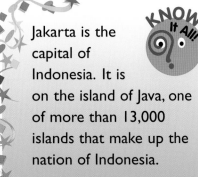

KNOW It All!

Jakarta is the capital of Indonesia. It is on the island of Java, one of more than 13,000 islands that make up the nation of Indonesia.

Homage to Cuauhtémoc

Dancers in feathered **headdresses** trimmed with beads and mirrors whirl and shake. The dancers move faster and faster until they suddenly stop. There is then a moment of silence.

The dance is part of a celebration held every year on August 21 in Mexico City to honor Cuauhtémoc (kwow TEHM ohk), the last Aztec Indian ruler of Mexico. The Aztecs were an American Indian people who ruled a mighty empire in Mexico during the 1400's and early 1500's. The Spaniards conquered the empire in 1521 and destroyed it.

Many people in Mexico today are related to the Aztecs. These people and other Mexicans honor Cuauhtémoc with a festival because of his bravery in defending the Aztecs. The festival includes readings of the story of his life and his fight against the Spanish and wonderful dances by large groups. Cuauhtémoc lived from about 1495 to 1525.

KNOW It All!!

Tenochtitlan (tay nohch TEE tlahn) was the capital of the Aztec Empire. It was located where Mexico City now stands.

Many Mexican place names, including Acapulco and Mexico itself, come from a form of the Aztec language. The English words *avocado*, *chocolate*, and *tomato* also come from this language.

In Mexico City, dancers in feathered headdresses perform at a celebration to honor Cuauhtémoc. He was the last Aztec Indian ruler of Mexico.

Homowo

Do you know any twins? Tell them there is a special day for them in Ghana (GAH nuh). Ghana lies in western Africa on the Atlantic Ocean. During the corn harvest in August or early September, people known as the Ga enjoy a harvest festival that includes a celebration of twins. On this day, twins who dress up in white clothing get special treats.

This woman and her daughter are carrying food for the festival.

The festival also includes dancing, singing, and parades. People wear their best clothing. All this fun continues for a week until Homowo Day. Then everyone opens up their home to friends and family and shares a wonderful harvest feast. There is fish from the sea and such traditional foods as special corn dough and **yams.** Like many holidays, Homowo is a time for enjoying the fruits of the harvest.

Homowo means "hooting at hunger." The day celebrates the first good harvest that the Ga people had after a time when many people went hungry long, long ago. It also marks the beginning of the new year for the Ga.

These children are taking part in the Homowo celebration.

These pictures represent some of the famous people born in September. The numbers tell you the days on which they were born. Look at the calendar on the following pages to find out more.

The Month of September

September is the ninth month of the year. The Roman name *September* comes from *septem,* the Latin word for "seven."

After the Romans switched September from the seventh to the ninth month, several Roman leaders tried to rename September. But they had no success.

Summer ends and autumn begins on September 22 or 23 in the northern half of the world. September is the time when many crops in the north are harvested. In the southern half of the world, winter is ending, and spring is just beginning.

19

September

Who Shares My Birthday?

7

Is your birthday in September? This calendar shows the names of some of the famous people born in September. What do you know about the people who share your birthday?

1

Edgar Rice Burroughs (1875) American author of "Tarzan" novels

Rocky Marciano (1923) American heavyweight boxing champion

2

Lydia Kamekeha Liliuokalani (1838) queen of Hawaii before it became a U.S. territory

Eugene Field (1850) American author and journalist who wrote "Wynken, Blynken, and Nod," a lullaby

7

Elizabeth I (1533) queen of England from 1558 to 1603

Grandma Moses (1860) American artist who started painting when she was over 70 years old. Her real name was Anna Moses

8

Richard I (1157) king of England from 1189 to 1199; known as Richard the Lion-Hearted

Jack Prelutsky (1937) American poet who wrote "The Headless Horseman Rides Tonight"

11

William Sydney Porter (1862) American author who wrote under the name O. Henry

James H. Jeans (1877) English physicist and mathematician

12

Irène Joliot-Curie (1897) French scientist and Nobel Prize winner

Jesse Owens (1913) American athlete and Olympic champion; one of the most famous athletes in sports history

13

Walter Reed (1851) American doctor who proved mosquitoes carry yellow fever

Arnold Schoenberg (1874) Austrian composer

Roald Dahl (1916) British author of *Charlie and the Chocolate Factory.*

14

Alexander von Humboldt (1769) German scientist and geographer

Margaret Sanger (1883) American nurse and founder of Planned Parenthood

19

Lajos Kossuth (1802) Hungarian patriot who led the revolt for Hungarian independence in 1840's

Rachel Field (1894) American author; won Newbery Medal for *Hitty, Her First Hundred Years*

20

Elizabeth Kenny (1880) Australian nurse who helped victims of polio

Jelly Roll Morton (1890) American composer of ragtime and jazz music

16

25

William H. Hughes (1862) prime minister of Australia during World War I

Sir Robert Muldoon (1921) prime minister of New Zealand from 1975 to 1984

26

Johnny Appleseed (1774) American pioneer planter of apple trees; real name was John Chapman

George Gershwin (1898) American composer; known for *Rhapsody in Blue*

27

Samuel Adams (1722) American patriot

Louis Botha (1862) first prime minister of South Africa

Thomas Nast (1840) American cartoonist who did sketches of Santa Claus

28

Georges Clemenceau (1841) French statesman; helped lead France in World War I

Kate Douglas Wiggin (1856) American author of children's books

3

Louis Sullivan (1856) American architect; one of the greatest American architects of all time

Sir Macfarlane Burnet (1899) Australian doctor and expert in virus diseases

4

François-René de Chateaubriand (1768) French author whose life story is called *Memoirs from Beyond the Grave*

Richard Wright (1908) American author who wrote *Native Son*

5

Louis XIV (1638) king of France for 72 years

Johann Christian Bach (1735) German composer and organist

6

Marquis de Lafayette (1757) French soldier and statesman

John Dalton (1766) English chemist who formed a basic theory of chemistry

Jane Addams (1860) American social reformer

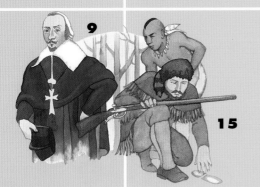

9

Cardinal Richelieu (1585) French statesman

Luigi Galvani (1737) Italian anatomist

Leo Tolstoy (1828) Russian writer of *War and Peace*

10

Thomas Sydenham (1624) English physician

Mungo Park (1771) Scottish-born explorer who explored the Niger River in Africa

Jose Feliciano (1945) American composer and guitarist

15

James Fenimore Cooper (1789) American author of *The Last of the Mohicans*

William H. Taft (1857) 27th president of the United States

Prince Henry (1984) British prince

16

H. A. Rey (1898) German-born illustrator of "Curious George" series

B. B. King (1925) American blues musician

David Copperfield (1956) American stage magician

17

Friedrich Augustin von Steuben (1730) German who fought in the Revolutionary War

Konstantin Tsiolkovsky (1857) Russian scientist and pioneer in space science

18

Samuel Johnson (1709) English author who is famous for writing a dictionary

John Diefenbaker (1895) 18th prime minister of Canada

21

Girolamo Savonarola (1452) Italian religious reformer

Louis Jolliet (1645) French-Canadian explorer who explored the Mississippi River

22

Lord Chesterfield (1694) English statesman and author

Michael Faraday (1791) English scientist who discovered how to create an electric current in wire

23

Augustus (63 B.C.) first Roman emperor

Louise Nevelson (1900) American sculptress who is known for using everyday objects in her work

24

F. Scott Fitzgerald (1896) American novelist and short-story writer

Jim Henson (1936) American puppeteer; creator of the "Muppets"

29

Horatio Nelson (1758) Britain's greatest admiral

Lech Walesa (1943) first president of Poland after fall of Communism

30

Pompey (106 B.C.) Roman general and statesman

Hans Wilhelm Geiger (1882) German inventor of the Geiger counter

This girl in Singapore is kneeling at an altar in honor of her ancestors during the Feast of the Hungry Ghosts.

Floating holiday

KNOW It All!

Singapore is a small island country in Asia. About three-fourths of the people of Singapore are Chinese.

Feast of the Hungry Ghosts

Have you ever heard of ghost money or hungry ghosts? These things are part of the Feast of the Hungry Ghosts, a holiday celebrated by Chinese people in Singapore and other countries.

Chinese believe that the souls of the dead roam the earth during September. On a special day, people offer gifts to the spirits of their **ancestors**.

The gifts are mostly food, clothes, and play money called "ghost money." It is believed that if these things are burned, the spirits will get them. They will then have food to eat, clothes to wear, and money to spend.

Brazilian Independence Day

September
7

Pedro's face grew grim as he read messages that had just come from Portugal, which ruled Brazil. Pedro was the son of Portugal's king and the leader of Brazil's people. The messages told him that Portugal refused to listen to Brazil's pleas to change some harsh new laws.

Pedro threw down the messages and shouted, "Independence or death!" And the fight for independence began that day— September 7, 1822. Less than two years later, Brazil was a free country. Brasília, the capital of Brazil, has a big parade on September 7, when all Brazilians celebrate Independence Day.

KNOW It All!

Pedro was the first **emperor** of independent Brazil. He is known as Pedro the First.

Rosh Ha-Shanah and Yom Kippur

It is sunset. The rabbi blows the shofar (SHOH fahr)—a trumpet made from a ram's horn. The notes of the shofar ring out through the synagogue. Rosh Ha-Shanah (rahsh huh SHAH nuh) has begun.

Rosh Ha-Shanah means "beginning of the year." It is the Jewish New Year celebration, an important religious holiday.

During the next 10 days, **Jews** pray and express their **sorrow** for any wrongs they have done during the year. Rosh Ha-Shanah falls on the first day of the

Hebrew month of Tishri and lasts 1 or 2 days. It can come anywhere between September 5 and October 5.

The 10th day following Rosh Ha-Shanah is Yom Kippur (YAHM KIHP uhr), which means "Day of Atonement" (uh TOHN muhnt). Atonement means making up for anything bad you may have done.

Yom Kippur is the most important and holiest day of the Jewish year. Like all Jewish holy days, it begins at sunset. Most people go to a service at a synagogue in the evening and again the following day.

During Yom Kippur, many Jews do not eat or drink anything. At sunset, a blast on the shofar signals the end of Yom Kippur.

TRY THIS! 2

Make sweet apple slices for a "sweet year, with no sadness in it." First, wash an apple. Ask a grown-up to slice it. Arrange the slices on a plate around a small bowl of honey. Dip an apple slice into the honey and enjoy the sweet goodness.

Mexican Independence Days

Grimly, Father Hidalgo (ee DAHL goh), the priest of the little Mexican community of Dolores, tugged at the rope that rang the church bell. He was calling the people to church earlier than usual on this Sunday morning.

It was September 15, 1810, and Father Hidalgo was going to give a very different kind of sermon. He was going to call on the Mexican people to rise up and free themselves from Spain.

The speech Father Hidalgo gave that morning became known as *Grito de Dolores,* or "Cry of Dolores." It was the beginning of years of war. Father Hidalgo, who is often called the Father of Mexican Independence, didn't live to see an independent Mexico. He was killed in 1811, but Mexico won its independence in 1821.

September 16, the day after Father Hidalgo gave the Cry of Dolores, is celebrated along with September 15 as Mexico's Independence Days. During the first evening of the Independence Days, the president of Mexico repeats the Cry of Dolores. Then he rings the same church bell that Father Hidalgo rang. Bells throughout Mexico ring out in honor of a free Mexico.

Teacher's Day

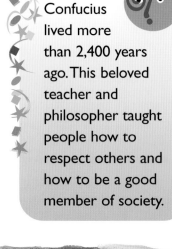

September
28

Do you have a special day to honor your teacher? In China, people honor all teachers with a national holiday called Teacher's Day.

On this day, people throughout China also celebrate the birthday of one of the greatest thinkers and teachers in Chinese history—Confucius (kuhn FYOO shuhs).

Some children may give their teachers cards or gifts on September 28, which is Teacher's Day and Confucius's Birthday. Also, some people in China hold a ceremony at dawn in Confucian temples. It includes music and special dances. People also put food offerings before the altar. This ceremony has been a Chinese **tradition** for more than 1,000 years.

KNOW It All!

Confucius lived more than 2,400 years ago. This beloved teacher and philosopher taught people how to respect others and how to be a good member of society.

Mid-Autumn Festival

The Mid-Autumn Festival was once a time of thanksgiving for the rice harvest. It falls in the middle of autumn on the night of the full moon in the old Chinese calendar. This usually occurs in August or September.

At midnight, Chinese people in many countries gather in parks to sing, dance, and look at the beautiful full moon while enjoying crisp pastries filled with sweet paste. It's the Mid-Autumn Festival, also known as the Moon Festival.

At this time of year, many people exchange moon cakes, round pastries filled with lotus seed, sesame, or another sweet paste. Many cakes have an egg yolk in them to make them look like the moon. Koreans also celebrate a Mid-Autumn Festival. During the festival, they may play sports and have picnics, or just rest and enjoy the fruits of the recent harvest.

These pictures represent some of the famous people born in October. The numbers tell you the days on which they were born. Look at the calendar on the following pages to find out more.

The Month of October

October is the 10th month of the year. This month got its name from *octo*, the Latin word for "eight." October was once the eighth month.

When the Romans made October the 10th month, rulers tried several times to rename this month in honor of certain **emperors** or members of their families. But the people continued to call this month October.

In parts of the northern half of the world, the first frost usually occurs in October. Leaves change to brilliant colors. In parts of the southern half of the world, the weather is just beginning to get warm.

23

October

Who Shares My Birthday?

7

Is your birthday in October? This calendar shows the names of some of the famous people born in October. What do you know about the people who share your birthday?

1
Annie Wood Besant (1847) British woman who worked for social change

Jimmy Carter (1924) 39th president of the United States

Mark McGwire (1963) American home-run superstar

2
Mohandas K. Gandhi (1869) Indian political leader, known as the "Father of India"

Cordell Hull (1871) American statesman and Nobel Prize winner for peace efforts from 1933 to 1944

7
James Whitcomb Riley (1849) American known as the "Hoosier Poet"

Niels Bohr (1885) Danish physicist who won the 1922 Nobel Prize for physics

Yo Yo Ma (1955) American cello player

13

14

12
James Ramsay MacDonald (1866) First Labour Party prime minister of Britain in 1924

Ralph Vaughan Williams (1872) British composer

13
Rudolf Virchow (1821) German physician and scientist

Arna Bontemps (1902) American author; wrote on black history

Margaret Thatcher (1925) British prime minister from 1979 to 1990

14
Eamon De Valera (1882) American-born leader in Ireland's fight to win independence

Dwight D. Eisenhower (1890) 34th president of the United States

Lois Lenski (1893) American author and illustrator

15
Virgil (70 B.C.) Greatest poet of ancient Rome

Helen Hunt Jackson (1830) American author of *Ramona*

Sarah Ferguson (1959) duchess of York

18
Henri Bergson (1859) French philosopher and 1927 Nobel Prize winner for literature

Pierre E. Trudeau (1919) 22nd prime minister of Canada

19
John McLoughlin (1784) Canadian pioneer, known as the "Father of Oregon"

Miguel Angel Asturias (1899) Guatemalan author and diplomat who won the Nobel Prize

20
Sir Christopher Wren (1632) English architect

John Dewey (1859) American philosopher and educator

Mickey Mantle (1931) New York Yankee baseball star from 1951 to 1968

21
Hokusai (1760) Japanese artist famous for his landscape prints of Mount Fuji

Alfred Nobel (1833) Swedish chemist who invented dynamite and founded the Nobel Prizes

26
Mahalia Jackson (1911) American gospel singer

François Mitterrand (1916) president of France from 1981 to 1995

27
James Cook (1728) British navigator and explorer of the Pacific Ocean

Theodore Roosevelt (1858) 26th president of the United States

28
Jonas Salk (1914) American research scientist who developed a vaccine to fight polio

Bruce Jenner (1949) American Olympic decathlon winner

29
James Boswell (1740) Scottish author of *The Life of Samuel Johnson*

Jean Giraudoux (1882) French playwright; known for plays that protest war and greed

3

Eleonora Duse (1858) Italian actress; called "greatest of her time"

Carl von Ossietzky (1888) German journalist who won 1935 Nobel Prize

4

Rutherford B. Hayes (1822) 19th president of the United States

Frederic Remington (1861) American artist; known for paintings of the American West

Kenichi Fukui (1918) Japanese scientist who won 1981 Nobel Prize

5

Chester A. Arthur (1829) 21st president of the United States

Louise Fitzhugh (1928) American author of *Harriet the Spy*

Václav Havel (1936) Czech poet and politician

6

Jenny Lind (1820) Swedish singer who was one of the most famous singers of the 1800's

Thor Heyerdahl (1914) Norwegian anthropologist and author of *Kon-Tiki*

8

Eddie Rickenbacker (1890) American pilot in World War I

Paul Hogan (1939) Australian actor; known for *Crocodile Dundee*

Jesse Jackson (1941) American minister and civil rights leader

9

Camille Saint-Saëns (1835) French composer

John Lennon (1940) British musician who was one of the Beatles

10

Giuseppe Verdi (1813) Italian composer of operas

Fridtjof Nansen (1861) Norwegian explorer and statesman

Harold Pinter (1930) English playwright

11

Eleanor Roosevelt (1884) American humanitarian; wife of President Franklin D. Roosevelt

Jerome Robbins (1918) American ballet dancer and choreographer

16

Noah Webster (1758) American educator who compiled *Webster's Dictionary*

Oscar Wilde (1854) Irish author; noted for his wit

David Ben-Gurion (1886) Israel's first prime minister

17

Arthur Miller (1915) American playwright who won a Pulitzer Prize for *Death of a Salesman*

William Anders (1933) American astronaut and ambassador to Norway

22

Franz Liszt (1811) Hungarian composer and most celebrated pianist of his time

Robert Rauschenberg (1925) American artist known for combining styles and materials in his work

23

Gertrude Ederle (1906) American athlete, the first woman to swim the English Channel

Pelé (1940) Brazilian soccer player; known as greatest soccer player of his time

24

Anton van Leeuwenhoek (1632) Dutch scientist

Sarah Josepha Hale (1788) American editor who wrote "Mary Had a Little Lamb"

Steven Kellogg (1941) American illustrator of *How Much Is a Million?*

25

Johann Strauss, Jr. (1825) Austrian composer known as the "Waltz King"

Pablo Picasso (1881) Spanish artist; founder of cubist style

Richard Byrd (1888) American admiral and polar explorer

30

John Adams (1735) 2nd president of the United States

Eric A. Kimmel (1946) American author of "Anansi the Spider" series

31

Jan Vermeer (1632) Dutch painter

Juliette Low (1860) founder of the Girl Scouts of America

National Day

With a rat-a-tat-tat of drums and a blare of bugles, rows of soldiers march smartly down the street. Overhead, a group of warplanes roars across the sky. Later, fireworks will light up the night sky. It's National Day in Nigeria.

Nigeria is on the west coast of Africa. Until 1960, Nigeria was part of the British Commonwealth. Then, on October 1, 1960, Great Britain granted Nigeria its independence. Nigeria adopted a green and white flag. The green is for agriculture and the white for unity and peace.

October 1 is a national holiday that Nigerians celebrate with great joy.

Gandhi's Birthday

In India, a wise and holy person is called a mahatma (muh HAHT muh). The word means "great soul." The greatest mahatma of all was Mohandas Karamchand Gandhi.

As a leader, Gandhi was against violence. He believed that how we behave is more important than what we succeed in doing. He won many followers.

Gandhi worked many years for India's freedom from Great Britain. His dream finally came true on August 15, 1947.

India celebrates the birthday of the great leader on October 2. In his honor, many people walk from far across India to the place where his body was **cremated**.

People gather at Gandhi's memorial to honor this "great soul" on his birthday.

151

Columbus Day

Over 500 years ago, Christopher Columbus was sure he could reach the Indies—Japan and China—by sailing west across the Atlantic Ocean. Others said, no, it couldn't be done. They thought it was too far.

Columbus thought that the Atlantic Ocean was very narrow. Others argued that the distance to Japan was four times greater than Columbus thought. But the

In the United States, Columbus Day is celebrated on the second Monday of October. Because Columbus sailed under the Spanish flag, people in Spain also celebrate Columbus Day. But Columbus wasn't Spanish. He was Italian. He was born in Genoa, Italy, and so Italians also celebrate Columbus Day. People in many Central and South American countries honor Columbus on October 12 because he also "discovered" their lands.

KNOW It All!

king and queen of Spain gave Columbus the money and ships he needed. If Columbus was right, Spain would be rich.

Columbus sailed from Palos, Spain, on August 3, 1492. He had three ships, the *Santa Maria*, the *Niña*, and the *Pinta*. The ships moved through a seemingly endless sea. Many weeks passed. The frightened sailors demanded that Columbus turn back, but he insisted that they continue sailing.

Finally, on October 12, 1492, they saw land. Columbus thought he had reached the Indies. But instead, he had reached the "New World." Columbus's voyage made America known to the people of Europe. This truly changed the world. That is why Columbus is honored.

Divali

It is late autumn in India, the day before Divali (dih VAH lee), or the Festival of Lights. In many homes, the children are busy making special holiday lamps. They fill little clay bowls with mustard oil. Into the oil, they put a little wick made of cotton. These lamps are a very important part of Divali. They are lit on the fourth day of this five-day festival.

During Divali, many palaces and other buildings in India are outlined with strings of electric lights.

In preparation for the holiday, families hang garlands of flowers over the door and prepare sweet cakes and candies.

The next day—Divali—everyone gets up early. The day is spent visiting relatives. There are lots of good things to eat and gifts to be exchanged. There may also be a visit to a street fair, where the children can go on rides and watch fireworks.

Before sunset, each family sets out its Divali lamps. All over the countryside the little lights glow, like stars brought down from the sky.

On Divali, Hindus welcome Lakshmi, the goddess of wealth and good luck.

According to **Hindu** beliefs, the Divali lamps will help guide Lakshmi (LAHK shmee), the goddess of wealth and good luck. She will fly down to earth and visit each house where the lamps are twinkling. Then, the family in that house will be blessed with good luck for a whole year.

155

United Nations Day

Can you think of a group that works for peace all over the world? One of the world's most important peacemakers is the United Nations (UN).

The United Nations was started on October 24, 1945. It began just after World War II (1939-1945). More people died in that war than in any other war in history. Many people agreed that such a war must never happen again. So they started a group that now has more than 180 countries working for peace.

Some children in the United States help raise money for the United Nations Children's Fund (UNICEF) every year on October 31. This day is Halloween, and the children collect money while **trick-or-treating.** UNICEF uses the money to provide food, medical care, and other services for poor children throughout the world.

KNOW It All!

A United Nations Day parade marches
through Yap Islands Village.

Today, the United Nations tries to solve
problems around the world before they
lead to war. It also helps people with
farming and building, and it helps many
countries improve their education and
health-care programs.

To honor the United Nations and its
work, many people celebrate United
Nations Day on October 24. Around the
world, people have peace marches, sports
events, exhibits, musical performances,
and special talks about UN programs.

These pictures represent some of the famous people born in November. The numbers tell you the days on which they were born. Look at the calendar on the following pages to find out more.

The Month of November

November is the eleventh month of the year. In ancient Roman times, November was the ninth month of the year. This month got its name from *novem*, the Latin word for "nine." And the name was never changed.

In the northern half of the world, many places are cold in November. In parts of the north, the trees are bare, and the dead leaves on the earth have lost the beautiful colors of October. In the southern half of the world, it is getting warmer in many places.

22

November

Who Shares My Birthday?

2

Is your birthday in November? This calendar shows the names of some of the famous people born in November. What do you know about the people who share your birthday?

1
Benvenuto Cellini (1500) Italian goldsmith and sculptor

Carlos Saavedra Lamas (1878) Argentinian statesman; Nobel Peace Prize winner

2
James K. Polk (1795) 11th president of the United States

Warren G. Harding (1865) 29th president of the United States

k. d. lang (1961) Canadian pop singer

7
Marie Sklodowska Curie (1867) Polish-born physicist who won Nobel Prize for chemistry in 1911

Joan Sutherland (1926) Australian opera star

8
Edmond Halley (1656) British astronomer for whom Halley's Comet is named

Margaret Mitchell (1900) American author of *Gone with the Wind*, a Civil War story

13
James C. Maxwell (1831) Scottish physicist and teacher

Robert Louis Stevenson (1850) Scottish author of *Treasure Island*

14
Jawaharlal Nehru (1889) first prime minister of India

Edward White (1930) American astronaut; first man to walk in space

Prince Charles (1948) heir to the British throne

15
William Pitt (1708) British statesman

William Herschel (1738) English astronomer

Georgia O'Keeffe (1887) American painter

Hussein I (1935) king of Jordan from 1952 to 1999

16
Louis H. Fréchette (1839) Canadian writer of lyric poetry

W. C. Handy (1873) American songwriter and bandleader; known as "Father of the Blues"

19
James A. Garfield (1831) 20th president of the United States

Indira Gandhi (1917) first woman prime minister of India; served from 1966 to 1977 and from 1980 to 1984

20
Sir Wilfrid Laurier (1841) 8th prime minister of Canada

Selma Lagerlöf (1858) Swedish writer who won 1909 Nobel Prize

Edwin Hubble (1889) American astronomer

17   18
19

25
Lope de Vega (1562) Spanish playwright

Marc Brown (1946) American author and illustrator of "Arthur" series

26
Mary E. Walker (1832) American Civil War doctor; won the Medal of Honor

Charles M. Schulz (1922) American cartoonist; creator of "Peanuts"

27
Chaim Weizmann (1874) Israeli statesman and first president of Israel

Kevin Henkes (1960) American author and illustrator of *A Weekend with Wendell*

28
William Blake (1757) English poet and painter

Stefan Zweig (1881) important Austrian author of 1900's

Ed Young (1931) American illustrator

3

Stephen Austin (1793) American pioneer in Texas

Karl Baedeker (1801) famous German publisher of travel books

Vilhjalmur Stefansson (1879) Canadian author and Arctic explorer

4

Will Rogers (1879) American cowboy who became famous as a humorist and social critic

Didier Ratsiraka (1936) president of Madagascar

5

Franz Gruber (1787) Austrian musician who wrote "Silent Night"

Eugene V. Debs (1855) American labor leader

Will Durant (1885) American philosopher, educator, and historian

6

John Philip Sousa (1854) American bandmaster

Ignace Jan Paderewski (1860) Polish pianist, composer, and statesman

9

Benjamin Banneker (1731) American astronomer and mathematician

Florence Rena Sabin (1871) American scientist

Lois Ehlert (1934) American author and illustrator of *Color Zoo*

10

Martin Luther (1483) German religious leader

William Hogarth (1697) English painter

Sir John S. D. Thompson (1844) 5th prime minister of Canada

11

Fyodor Dostoevsky (1821) Russian author who wrote *The Brothers Karamazov*

Kurt Vonnegut (1922) American author who wrote *Cat's Cradle*

12

Baha'u'llah (1817) Persian founder of the Baha'i Faith

Grace Kelly (1929) princess of Monaco who was a Hollywood actress

Sammy Sosa (1969) American home-run superstar

15

14

17

Bernard Montgomery (1887) British general and field marshal in World War II

18

Louis Daguerre (1787) French inventor of early type of photograph

Sir William S. Gilbert (1836) English playwright and songwriter

21

Voltaire (1694) French author and philosopher; his real name was François Marie Arouet

Sir Samuel Cunard (1787) Canadian shipowner who started regular mail service across the Atlantic Ocean

22

Abigail Adams (1744) wife of President John Adams and mother of President John Quincy Adams

George Eliot (1819) English author

Charles De Gaulle (1890) patriot, soldier, and president of France

23

Franklin Pierce (1804) 14th president of the United States

Sir Gilbert Parker (1862) Canadian author of historical stories

José Clemente Orozco (1883) Mexican painter known for historical murals

24

Junípero Serra (1713) Spanish missionary who founded the first mission in California

Zachary Taylor (1784) 12th president of the United States

Henri de Toulouse-Lautrec (1864) French painter

29

Andres Bello (1781) Venezuelan diplomat

Louisa May Alcott (1832) American author of *Little Women*

Madeleine L'Engle (1918) American author who wrote *A Wrinkle in Time*

30

Jonathan Swift (1667) English author of *Gulliver's Travels*

Mark Twain (1835) American author; his real name was Samuel Clemens

29

30

Mexican families gather in cemeteries during the Day-of-the-Dead celebration. They decorate graves with beautiful flowers and candles.

Mexican sugar skulls

November 1

Day-of-the-Dead

Children bite into crisp sugar skulls. People dressed as skeletons dance down the streets. **Cemeteries** light up with the warm glow of candles. It's November 1, the start of the two-day Day-of-the-Dead celebration in Mexico.

TRY THIS! 1

You can make a Day-of-the-Dead decoration out of self-hardening clay.

Roll one color of clay into an egg shape about the size of your fist. Lay it on its side and push down gently so that it has a flat bottom. Gently mold it into the shape seen to the right and use a pencil to make holes for the face. Decorate the skull with different colors of clay. Let the skull dry one or two days on a wire rack. When the skull is hard, display it on a windowsill.

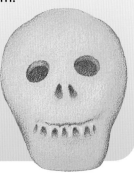

On this day, many Mexicans believe that the spirits of the dead return to visit their homes. Processions are held through towns. Families and friends gather in cemeteries and clean and decorate gravesites with flowers to welcome the spirits.

People picnic together and enjoy such special foods as sugar skulls and breads baked with a plastic skeleton hidden in them. It is a time when people remember the dead and celebrate life.

KNOW It All!!

Can you think of other holidays on which people leave out food or lanterns for returning spirits of the dead (see pages 117 and 138)?

These people gather in the evening at a cemetery on the Day-of-the-Dead.

Seven-Five-Three

November
15

According to an old **tradition** in Japan, girls who are 3 or 7 years old and boys who are 5 are thought to be especially fortunate. So on November 15, families who have children of these ages take part in a festival called Seven-Five-Three.

On this day, the families go to a **shrine,** or place of worship. There, they give thanks for the good health of the children. They also ask for future health and happiness for the children.

Outside the shrine, parents buy candy and toys for the children. Later, the children give some of their candy to visiting friends and relatives. In return, they are often given gifts.

On this day, the children dress in their finest clothes. Some wear brightly colored robes called kimonos. And every child has a long, decorated paper bag for candy and toys. Each bag is decorated with colorful pictures, usually of a pine tree, a tortoise, and a crane. These are symbols of youth and long life.

Remembrance Day

November 11

For more than four years, the war raged on. Then, at 11:00 a.m. on November 11, 1918, the guns stopped firing. World War I was over on the eleventh hour of the eleventh day of the eleventh month. An armistice— an agreement to end the war—had been signed.

November 11 became Armistice Day, a day on which many nations honor those who died for their country. In France, it is still called Armistice Day. In Canada, Australia, and New Zealand, November 11 is Remembrance Day and honors all people who have died in war. The United Kingdom celebrates Remembrance Day on the Sunday closest to November 11.

In 1954, Armistice Day was changed to Veterans Day in the United States. It became a time to honor all the men and women who have served in the nation's armed forces.

Each year, at Arlington National Cemetery in Virginia, there are special ceremonies. They begin with two minutes of silence, followed by a bugler playing "Taps." A wreath is placed at the Tomb of the Unknowns. The tomb honors members of the U.S. armed forces who have died in war. The red poppy is the symbol of Remembrance Day.

On Remembrance Day in Canada, people visit war memorials and leave flowers in memory of all the Canadians who died for their country.

Thanksgiving

Floating holiday

Mm-mmmm! Smell the turkey cooking! It's Thanksgiving Day and company's coming! In the United States and Canada, this is a special holiday. Families and friends gather to eat and give thanks for their blessings.

Thanksgiving Day is really a harvest festival. That's why it is celebrated in late fall, after the crops have been gathered.

The Pilgrims of New England celebrated the first harvest thanksgiving. They were early English settlers who came to America in 1620 looking for a better life. The Pilgrims had a hard time during their first year, many of them dying during the first winter. But the next year, in 1621, they had a good harvest. So, their governor declared a three-day feast.

The Pilgrims invited American Indian friends to join them for the special feast. In time, other colonies began to celebrate a day of thanksgiving.

Today, people in the United States celebrate Thanksgiving on the fourth Thursday in November. Canadians celebrate Thanksgiving Day on the second Monday in October.

KNOW It All!

For thousands of years, people in many parts of the world have held harvest festivals. The Chinese Mid-Autumn Festival was once a celebration of the end of the rice harvest (see page 145). African Americans celebrate the African harvest at the end of December (see page 182).

These pictures represent some of the famous people born in December. The numbers tell you the days on which they were born. Look at the calendar on the following pages to find out more.

The Month of December

December is the twelfth month of the year. In ancient Roman times, December was the 10th month of the year. So the month got its name from *decem*, the Latin word for "ten."

In the northern half of the world, winter begins on December 21 or 22. There, it is the shortest day of the year. At the same time, summer begins in the southern half of the world. There, it is the longest day of the year.

8

December

Who Shares My Birthday?

Is your birthday in December? This calendar shows the names of some of the famous people born in December. What do you know about the people who share your birthday?

5

1

Madame Tussaud (1761) Swiss wax modeler famous for her wax museum in London

Jan Brett (1949) American author and illustrator of *Fritz and the Beautiful Horses*

2

Georges Seurat (1859) French artist who started a way of painting called pointillism

Maria Callas (1923) American opera singer

Monica Seles (1973) Yugoslavian-born tennis champion

7

Willa Cather (1873) American writer known for novels about Nebraska and the Southwest

Joyce Kilmer (1886) American poet best known for "Trees"

8

Eli Whitney (1765) American inventor of the cotton gin

Padraic Colum (1881) Irish poet and author of young people's books

Diego Rivera (1886) Mexican artist known for murals that portray Mexican life and history

12

John Jay (1745) American diplomat and first chief justice of the United States

Gustave Flaubert (1821) French author

Edvard Munch (1863) Norwegian artist who painted *The Scream*

13

Heinrich Heine (1797) German poet who became one of the most popular writers in German literature

Emily Carr (1871) Canadian painter and writer

16

21

18

18

Francis Ferdinand (1863) archduke of Austria whose murder started World War I

Benjamin O. Davis, Jr. (1912) first African American major general

Steven Spielberg (1947) American movie director

19

Albert Michelson (1852) American physicist and Nobel Prize winner

Leonid I. Brezhnev (1906) leader of the former Soviet Union in the 1960's and 1970's

20

Harvey Firestone (1868) American founder of Firestone Tire & Rubber Company

Sir Robert Gordon Menzies (1894) prime minister of Australia from 1939 to 1941 and from 1949 to 1966

21

Saint Thomas Becket (1118?) English archbishop of Canterbury

Benjamin Disraeli (1804) prime minister of Great Britain in 1868 and from 1874 to 1880

Albert Payson Terhune (1872) American author of stories about dogs

26

Thomas Gray (1716) English poet; wrote "Elegy Written in a Country Churchyard"

George Dewey (1837) American admiral; hero of Spanish-American War

27

Louis Pasteur (1822) French scientist who discovered disease is spread by bacteria

Sir Mackenzie Bowell (1823) 6th prime minister of Canada

28

Earl (Fatha) Hines (1903) American jazz musician

Birendra Bir Bikram Shah Dev (1945) king of Nepal who oversaw change of government in 1990

29

Andrew Johnson (1808) 17th president of the United States

William Ewart Gladstone (1809) British prime minister

Woodrow Wilson (1856) 28th president of the United States

3

George McClellan (1826) Union Army general in the Civil War

Joseph Conrad (1857) Polish-born author who wrote some of the greatest novels in English

4

Thomas Carlyle (1795) Scottish author of essays and French and English history

Edith Cavell (1865) World War I English nurse; Mount Edith Cavell in Alberta, Canada, is named for her

5

Martin Van Buren (1782) 8th president of the United States

George Armstrong Custer (1839) American cavalry officer defeated at Little Bighorn

Walt Disney (1901) American creator of Mickey Mouse

6

Warren Hastings (1732) British businessman and statesman who was first governor general of India

Ira Gershwin (1896) American lyricist who worked with brother George Gershwin

9

John Milton (1608) English poet

Joel Chandler Harris (1848) American author of the "Uncle Remus" stories

Jean de Brunhoff (1899) French author and illustrator of "Babar the Elephant" series

10

César Franck (1822) Belgian-born composer of music for piano and orchestra

Emily Dickinson (1830) American poet; one of the most gifted poets in American literature

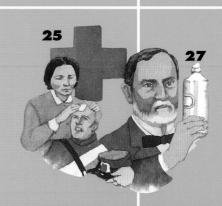

10

11

Hector Berlioz (1803) French composer, conductor, critic, and writer

Annie Jump Cannon (1863) American astronomer who cataloged hundreds of stars

14

Nostradamus (1503) French physician known for astrological predictions

Tycho Brahe (1546) Danish astronomer who made important observations on motions of planets

15

Maxwell Anderson (1888) American playwright and 1933 Pulitzer Prize winner

J. Paul Getty (1892) American billionaire who made his fortune in the oil business

16

Jane Austen (1775) English author of *Pride and Prejudice* and other books

Margaret Mead (1901) American anthropologist and author

17

John Greenleaf Whittier (1807) American poet; known for poems that attack slavery

William Lyon MacKenzie King (1874) 12th, 14th, and 16th prime minister of Canada

22

James Oglethorpe (1696) English founder and first governor of the colony of Georgia

Giacomo Puccini (1858) Italian opera composer who wrote *La Bohème*

23

Richard Arkwright (1732) British inventor of a machine to make thread

Akihito (1933) emperor of Japan who broke an old tradition by marrying a "commoner"

24

George I (1845) Greek king who supported bringing back the Olympic Games

Johnny Gruelle (1880) American author and illustrator of "Raggedy Ann and Andy" series

25

Isaac Newton (1642) English mathematician and scientist who developed the theory of gravity

Clara Barton (1821) founder of the American Red Cross

30

Rudyard Kipling (1865) English author of *The Jungle Book* and *Just So Stories*

31

Jacques Cartier (1491?) French explorer who led the first European expedition up the St. Lawrence River

Henri Matisse (1869) French painter

25

27

Feast of Saint Nicholas

Long ago, a very kind man lived in what is now the country of Turkey. This man was a bishop named Nicholas. According to stories about him, Nicholas often helped needy children.

Many years after his death, Nicholas was made a **saint**. He became the **patron saint** of children. Today, he is honored on December 6.

This day is a holiday in some European countries. On the night before, children put out their shoes. Early the next morning, they rush to see what Saint Nicholas left for them. According to **tradition,** good children receive gifts, and naughty children may get sticks.

KNOW It All!

Where did the name Santa Claus come from? The Dutch name for Saint Nicholas is Sinterklaas. And in English, this became Santa Claus. Dutch settlers in America continued to celebrate the Feast of Saint Nicholas. Later, stories about Santa Claus became part of the Christmas tradition (see pages 178-181).

Saint Nicholas arrives in the city of Amsterdam by boat.

On December 6, some European cities and towns also hold parades led by a figure dressed up as Saint Nicholas. He talks to children and often hands out small gifts.

Saint Nicholas always has a helper with him. Children are quite afraid of his helper because the helper keeps track of who was good and who was naughty. In the Netherlands, Saint Nicholas' helper is called Black Peter.

Hanukkah

Floating holiday

On the stove, crisp potato pancakes sputter in a skillet. In a corner, children spin square tops on the floor. On the table, candles twinkle in a candleholder. It's Hanukkah (HAH nu kah), the Jewish Feast of Lights, and it lasts eight days.

Hanukkah honors a marvelous event that happened more than 2,000 years ago. At that time, the **Jews** won their struggle for religious freedom by defeating the Syrians, who tried to make them give up their religion.

Hanukkah is a cheerful time. There may be a party. People enjoy such special holiday food as potato pancakes, called latkes. Gifts and contributions are often given to the poor.

Here is a brief story of the menorah. After their great victory over the Syrians, the Jews began cleaning the great Temple of Jerusalem. They wanted to light the holy lamps. But they could find only a tiny jar of the special oil they needed for the lamps. They were amazed when the jar provided them with enough oil for eight days.

The eight days of Hanukkah are in memory of the eight days the lamps stayed lit. A special symbol of Hanukkah is the eight-branched candleholder called the menorah. On each day of Hanukkah, the candles of the menorah are lit—one on the first day, two on the second, and so on. Many menorahs have a branch to hold a ninth candle used to light the other candles.

Each evening, families light some or all of the candles of the special eight-branched candleholder called a **menorah** (muh NAWR uh). Some families sing songs and play games. Many families also give their children gifts.

Hanukkah starts on the eve of the 25th day of the Hebrew month of Kislev, which falls in November or December. The word *Hanukkah* means "dedication."

This family is lighting their menorah on the first day of Hanukkah.

Christmas

For **Christians** all over the world, December 25 is an important, happy day. It is Christmas, the day that celebrates the birth of Jesus Christ.

Many Christmas customs are based on the birth of Christ. People give each other presents because the Three Kings brought presents to the baby Jesus. Christians sing songs, called **carols**, that tell about Christ's birth. And they put up scenes of Jesus's birth, with figures of the shepherds, the Three Kings, and animals around the tiny baby.

People in many countries act out the story of Jesus's birth during Christmas.

This beautiful nativity scene decorates a church in the Philippines.

Some customs probably came from harvest festivals that took place in December around Christmastime. The Roman harvest festival may have inspired feasting and having parties. The custom of burning Yule logs came from the Northern European harvest festival known as Yule.

Other customs are newer traditions. Decorating Christmas trees probably came from Germany. Sending Christmas cards came from England.

KNOW It All!
The name for this holiday, *Christmas*, is a short form of *Christ's Mass*, an old name for this day. It means a *Mass*, or church service, in honor of Christ.

A visit with Santa is a Christmas treat for children throughout the world.

Today, one of the most popular Christmas customs is giving gifts. In the United States and Canada, a magical person named Santa Claus brings presents. Santa wears red clothes trimmed with white fur, and he has a snow-white beard and mustache. Santa drives through the sky in a sleigh drawn by eight reindeer. He slips down the chimney, leaves gifts, and goes on his way again.

In England, the gift bringer is called Father Christmas. He looks much like Santa Claus, but he has a longer coat and a longer beard. In Germany, Costa Rica, Colombia, and parts of Mexico, children get presents from the Christ child.

In Sweden, gifts and goodies are brought by a Christmas elf. This little gnome has a sleigh that is pulled by two goats.

Both Father Christmas and Santa Claus are popular in Australia and New Zealand. But in these countries, December comes during the summer. So many people celebrate by going on a picnic or having fun at the beach.

the Swedish Christmas elf

Children in many cultures get gifts from Father Christmas.

Kwanzaa

How does your family celebrate its cultural heritage? If you are an African American, you may celebrate Kwanzaa (KWAHN zuh). Kwanzaa celebrates a traditional African harvest festival. It is also a celebration of the rich cultural roots of African Americans.

Kwanzaa takes place from December 26 to January 1. Each evening during Kwanzaa, the family lights a candle in a special candleholder called a **kinara** (kee NAH rah). Each candle stands for one of the seven goals of Kwanzaa. These goals are ways that people can work together to build their communities and nourish pride and creativity among African Americans.

A karamu (kah RAH moo) celebration occurs at the end of the holiday.

Near the end of the holiday, the community gathers for a feast. There is African food and music and dancing.

Rizal Day

Books and cartoons are filled with heroes. But real live people are known for great deeds, too. Most countries have heroes who helped their nation in one way or another. One hero of the Philippines is José Rizal (hoh ZAY ree ZAHL).

Rizal helped the people of the Philippines fight for their freedom from Spain. The Spanish thought he wanted to cause a **revolution.** So they shot and killed him on December 30, 1896. The United States took control of the Philippines in 1898. The Philippines finally gained complete independence in 1946.

December 30 is now a national holiday in the Philippines. It is called Rizal Day. On this day, the Philippine president lays a wreath on a monument to Rizal in Manila.

TRY THIS!
1

Who is your hero? It could be a famous person or someone you know. What makes this person special? Write a story or draw a picture about that person. Show why that person is special.

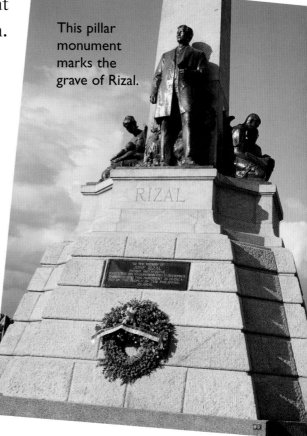

This pillar monument marks the grave of Rizal.

Glossary

Here are some of the words you read in this book. Many of them may be new to you. Some are hard to pronounce. But since you will see them again, they are good words to know. Next to each word, you will see how to say it correctly: **cemeteries** (SEHM uh TEHR eez). The part shown in small capital letters is said a little more loudly than the rest of the word. The part in large capital letters is said the loudest. Under each word are one or two sentences that tell what the word means.

A

ancestors (AN sehs tuhrz)
Ancestors are the people from whom one is descended. Grandparents and their parents are examples of one's ancestors.

B

bar mitzvah (bahr MIHTS vuh)
A bar mitzvah is the Jewish ceremony of confirmation for boys. The words mean "son of the commandment."

bat mitzvah (baht MIHTS vuh)
A bat mitzvah is the Jewish ceremony of confirmation for girls. The words mean "daughter of the commandment."

bonfires (BAHN fyrz)
Bonfires are large fires that are built outdoors.

Buddhists (BOO dihsts)
Buddhists are people who follow the religion called Buddhism.

C

carols (KAR uhls)
Carols are joyous songs that are generally religious. One common type of carol tells about Christ's birth.

cemeteries (SEHM ih TEHR eez)
Cemeteries are places for burying the dead.

Christians (KRIHS chuhns)
Christians are people who follow the religion called Christianity.

Confucius (kuhn FYOO shuhs)
Confucius was one of the greatest teachers in Chinese history. People who belong to the religion called Confucianism follow his teachings.

cremate (KREE mayt)
To cremate is to burn a body to ashes instead of burying it.

E

emperor (EHM puhr uhr)
An emperor is a man who rules an empire.

Epiphany (ih PIHF uh nee)
Epiphany is a holiday that once celebrated Christ's birth. The word epiphany means "appearance."

F

fasting (FAST ihng)
Fasting is not eating, eating less than usual, or not eating certain foods for a certain length of time.

Filipinos (fihl uh PEE nohs)
Filipinos are the people of the Philippines.

founder (FOWN duhr)
A founder is a person who starts something, such as an organization or a religion.

frankincense (FRANG kihn sehns)
Frankincense is a fragrant gum from certain trees. It smells sweet and spicy when burned.

H

hajj (haj)
A hajj is the journey that Muslims make to Mecca, the holy city of Islam in western Saudi Arabia.

headdresses (HEHD drehs ehz)
Headdresses are coverings or decorations for the head.

Hindus (HIHN dooz)
Hindus are people who follow the religion called Hinduism.

homage (HAHM ihj)
Homage is great honor or respect shown to someone.

I

incense (IHN sehns)
Incense is a sweet-smelling oil or powder that is burned for its pleasant fragrance.

J

Jews (jooz)
Jews are people who follow the religion called Judaism.

K

kilts (kihlts)
Kilts are pleated tartan (plaid) skirts worn by Scottish people.

kinara (kee NAH ruh)
A kinara is a special candleholder used during the celebration of Kwanzaa. The kinara holds seven candles, one for each day of Kwanzaa.

M

Maori (MAH oh ree)
The Maori are a people who were among the first people to live in New Zealand.

Mardi Gras (MAHR dee grah)
Mardi Gras is a festival. The name is French for "Fat Tuesday." It comes from the old custom of parading a fat ox through the streets of Paris on this day to remind the people not to eat meat during Lent.

matzah (MAHT suh)
Matzah is unleavened bread that is like large crackers. It is eaten during the Jewish holiday of Passover.

Maypole (MAY pohl)
A Maypole is a tall pole decorated with flowers and ribbons. People dance around it during a spring celebration in May.

menorah (muh NAWR uh)
A menorah is an eight-branched or nine-branched candleholder. It is a special symbol of Hanukkah.

Muslims (MUHZ luhmz)
are people who follow the Islamic religion.

myrrh (mur)
Myrrh is a fragrant substance used in perfumes and incense.

N

Northern Hemisphere (NAWR thuhrn HEHM uh sfihr)
The Northern Hemisphere is the northern half of the earth, from the North Pole to the equator.

P

papier mâché (PAY puhr muh SHAY)
Papier mâché is a special mixture of paper and flour or glue. It is built up in layers while it is wet and hardens when it is dry.

patron saint (PAY truhn saynt)
A patron saint is the heavenly guardian of a person, church, city, or nation.

pilgrimage (PIHL gruh mihj)
A pilgrimage is a journey to a holy place. People of many religious faiths make pilgrimages.

prophet (PRAHF iht)
A prophet is a special religious teacher.

Q

Quran (ku RAHN)
The Quran is the holy book of the Muslims.

R

revolution (rehv uh LOO shuhn)
A revolution is a revolt against the government of a country.

S

saints (saynts)
Saints are holy people.

shamrocks (SHAM rahks)
Shamrocks are bright green leaves that have three parts like a clover.

shrine (shryn)
A shrine is a holy place for worship. It may also be a place or object that is sacred because of its history.

sorrow (SAHR oh)
Sorrow is sadness.

Southern Hemisphere (SUHTH uhrn HEHM uh sfihr)
The Southern Hemisphere is the southern half of the earth, from the equator to the South Pole.

T

traditions (truh DIHSH uhnz)
Traditions are beliefs or customs that are handed down from parents to children. Children may learn traditions from parents who talk about them or practice them.

trick-or-treating (trihk uhr TREE tihng)
Trick-or-treating is a custom that children in the United States may practice on Halloween. They dress up in costumes and go to the homes of friends, neighbors, and family for candy and other treats.

Y

yams (yamz)
Yams are starchy roots that are like potatoes.

Index

This index is an alphabetical list of important topics covered in this book. It will help you find information given in both words and pictures. To help you understand what an entry means, there is sometimes a helping word in parentheses, for example, **Aborigines** (people). If there is information in both words and pictures, you will see the words *with pictures* in parentheses after the page number. If there is only a picture, you will see the word *picture* in parentheses after the page number.

190

Illustration Acknowledgments

The Publishers of *Childcraft* gratefully acknowledge the courtesy of the following illustrators, photographers, agencies, and organizations for illustrations in this volume. When all the illustrations for a sequence of pages are from a single source, the inclusive page numbers are given. Credits should be read from top to bottom, left to right, on their respective pages. All illustrations are the exclusive property of the publishers of *Childcraft* unless names are marked with an asterisk(*).

Cover	Fireworks in Sydney—© Manfred Gottschalk, Tom Stack & Associates*; Girl blowing out birthday candles—© Michael Keller, The Stock Market*; Folklorico dancers—© Robert Daemmrich, Tony Stone Images*
Back Cover	© Robert Daemmrich, Tony Stone Images*
1	© Michael Keller, The Stock Market*; © Robert Daemmrich, Tony Stone Images*
2-3	Roberta Polfus
4-5	Gwen Connelly
6-7	Jon Goodell; © CHILDCRAFT photo by Tomokazu Imai*; Yoshi Miyake; Gwen Connelly
8-13	Gwen Connelly
14-15	Dale Paysen; Gwen Connelly
16-17	© Joe Viesti*; Gwen Connelly
18-19	Gwen Connelly
20-21	Angela Adams; Gwen Connelly; Yoshi Miyake
22-23	Angela Adams
24-25	Gwen Connelly
26-27	AP/Wide World*; © Tournament of Roses*
28-29	Gwen Connelly; Roberta Polfus; © Michael A. Vaccaro, Louis Mercier*
30-31	© Annie Griffiths Belt, Corbis*; © Georg Gerster, Photo Researchers*
32-33	© Robert Frerck*
34-35	Gwen Connelly
36-37	© Consolidated News/Archive Photos*; AP/Wide World*
38-39	Angela Adams
40-41	Lydia West; Angela Adams; Angela Adams
42-43	Ben Mahan
44-45	Jon Goodell; Ben Mahan
46-47	Roberta Polfus
48-49	© Olivia Garcia, Impact Visuals*
50-51	© Mark Downey*; Jon Goodell; © Claus Meyer, Black Star*
52-53	Jon Goodell; © Fred J. Maroon, Louis Mercier*
54-55	AP/Wide World*
56-57	Angela Adams
58-59	Angela Adams; Angela Adams; Angela Adams; Yoshi Miyake
60-61	© Orion Press*; © Margaret Woodbury Strong Museum, Rochester, N.Y.*; Lorraine Epstein; Gwen Connelly
62-63	© Joe Viesti*; Historical Picture Archive from Corbis*
64-65	© Joe Viesti*; Marc Brown; © Australian Picture Library*
66-67	© A. G. E. Fotostock*; Gwen Connelly
68-69	© Athens News Agency*
70-71	Angela Adams
72-73	Angela Adams; Yoshi Miyake; Angela Adams; Angela Adams; Yoshi Miyake
74-75	Gwen Connelly; © CHILDCRAFT photo by Tomokazu Imai
76-77	Robert Polfus
78-79	Gwen Connelly; CHILDCRAFT photo by Gilbert Meyers; © James Suger, Woodfin Camp, Inc.*
80-81	Janet Palmer; © Bill Aron, Photo Researchers*; © Superstock*
82-83	Angela Adams
84-85	Angela Adams; Angela Adams; Yoshi Miyake; Angela Adams
86-87	© Van Hasselt, Sygma*
88-89	Roberta Polfus; © Steven Needham, Envision*
90-91	Roberta Polfus
92-93	Gwen Connelly; © Richard T. Nowitz*
94-95	Roberta Polfus; © Brent Jones*
96-97	Angela Adams; Angela Adams; Yoshi Miyake
98-99	Angela Adams
100-101	George Suyeoka
102-103	Karen Ackoff; © Ted Spiegel, Black Star*
104-105	© Ronnie Kaufman, The Stock Market*; Roberta Polfus
106-107	Roberta Polfus; © Kjell Johansson, Bildhuset*
108-109	Karen Ackoff; George Suyeoka
110-111	Angela Adams; Angela Adams; Yoshi Miyake
112-113	Yoshi Miyake; Angela Adams; Angela Adams
114-115	© S. S. Gifford, Images Finders*; © Wilton Abel*; Karen Ackoff
116-117	Marc Brown; © Sisse Gifford, Lensman*; © Tourou Nagashi, Haga Library Inc.*
118-119	French Government Tourist Office*; Roberta Polfus
120-121	Roberta Polfus
122-123	Angela Adams; Yoshi Miyake; Angela Adams; Angela Adams
124-125	Yoshi Miyake; Yoshi Miyake; Yoshi Miyake; Angela Adams
126-127	Roberta Polfus
128-129	Roberta Polfus; Daniel Brennan
130-131	© Victor Englebert*
132-133	© Jason Laure*
134-135	Yoshi Miyake; Angela Adams; Yoshi Miyake; Angela Adams
136-137	Angela Adams; Yoshi Miyake; Angela Adams
138-139	© Demetrio Carrasco, Tony Stone Images*; Gwen Connelly
140-141	George Suyeoka; CHILDCRAFT photo
142-143	Michael Hayes
144-145	Gwen Connelly; Steven Brayfield; Gwen Connelly
146-147	Angela Adams; Yoshi Miyake; Angela Adams; Yoshi Miyake
148-149	Angela Adams
150-151	George Suyeoka; © Suraj N. Sharman, Dinodia Picture Agency*
152-153	Bill Ersland
154-155	© Dean Brown, Nancy Palmer Agency*; © J. H. C. Wilson, Robert Harding Picture Library*
156-157	© G. Lange, 99TNT/INICEF*; © Jack Fields, Corbis*
158-159	Angela Adams
160-161	Yoshi Miyake; Angela Adams; Yoshi Miyake; Angela Adams
162-163	© Joe Viesti; © Robert Frerck, Tony Stone Images*; Roberta Polfus; © Michael Townsent, Tony Stone Images*
164-165	© Orion Press*; Roberta Polfus
166-167	Roberta Polfus; © Koos Dykstra, Image Finders*; Roberta Polfus
168-169	Gwen Connelly; Ben Mahan
170-171	Yoshi Miyake; Angela Adams; Angela Adams; Yoshi Miyake
172-173	Angela Adams
174-175	© Kyrn Taconis, Magnum*; Gwen Connelly
176-177	Diana Uelinger; Ben Mahan
178-179	WORLD BOOK photo by Prime Inc.
180-181	WORLD BOOK photo by Dan Miller; Gwen Connelly
182-183	© Brent Jones*; © Paul Almasy, Corbis*